The 6-Pack Portfolio

How to Beat the Canadian Stock Market

Jason Fremlin

This book provides information that the author deems accurate. However, it is sold without the intent of providing individual investment advice to any one person or portfolio. Seek professional accounting, legal, and investment advice elsewhere. Historical performance figures are calculated using third party tools, and are not a guarantee of future success. The author claims no personal responsibility for any financial loss or liability from the direct or indirect application of the contents of this book.

ISBN: 1983979880
ISBN-13: 978-1983979880

DEDICATION

Dedicated to my grandfather Ron Fremlin, who sparked my love of investing as a boy. And to my wonderful young family – my wife Veronika and daughter Grace.

CONTENTS

FOREWORD

I do not have a fancy foreword from a billionaire, a celebrity, or a titan of the investment industry. I do not have any special qualifications, aside from perhaps an MBA degree. But that and $2 will get me a cup of coffee.

All I have done is manage to beat the performance of the stock market every single year. And within this book, I will show you exactly how I did it – and how you can do the same. This is not a get-rich-quick scheme, it's long-term wealth building based on logical selection of assets and companies.

Before you start reading, I will make the assumption that you know that the investment industry exists mainly for the purposes of enriching the investment industry. And that the person who cares most about your own financial well-being is yourself.

This book is not a sales pitch, as I receive no commissions or benefit from your following my recommendations. My only monetary gain is from your purchase of this book – for about the cost of buying me lunch. I hope you find value within these pages, and wish you good fortune!

Thanks for the lunch,
Jason Fremlin

INTRODUCTION

"You can't beat the market."

It is the rallying cry of investment philosophy in the 21st Century. And in many cases, with good reason. In the United States, where the largest amount of data is available, various studies show that only about 5% of money managers end up outperforming their benchmark over time. The underperformance of active management, along with enabling technology, has helped give rise to the trend of passive investment for the modern investor.

How does passive investment differ from active management? Well, if you enlist your broker, advisor, family member, or yourself for the task of picking a selection of individual stocks to own and trade directly, that is active management. Passive investment usually entails buying an investment product or combination of products that track their respective benchmarks. For instance, if you buy a fund that tracks the S&P 500, then you will indirectly own all 500 stocks in the benchmark, and your investment performance will follow accordingly.

Just how popular is passive investment nowadays? In 2016, investors in the United States pulled $285 billion out of actively managed funds, which corresponded with inflows of roughly equal amounts into passive funds. It is an unstoppable trend, and for the average investor south of the border, probably a good strategy. But if you bought this book, you are either from Canada, or are interested in investing in Canadian stocks. And I am here to tell you that the Canadian market lends itself better to stock-picking than indexing. Now why own individual stocks directly rather than just buying the whole Canadian market, via a TSX (Toronto Stock Exchange) index?

Because the TSX index is terrible.

Roughly 70% of the index is made up of companies in the Financial, Energy, and Materials sectors. Basically, this means that if you passively invest in Canada, the vast majority of your money will be tied up in the big banks and in companies that pull resources out of the ground. There are some good stocks within these sectors, but to have such a concentrated portfolio is not a sound strategy. We saw this in 2008, when the financial crisis hit and bank stocks led the market charge downwards. And from 2013 to the present time, commodity prices have suffered, eroding the value of the oil companies and miners that make up the Energy and Materials sectors in Canada. Simply put, investing passively in the S&P/TSX 60 or S&P/TSX Composite is a poor use of your hard-earned money.

For those of you looking to beat the market, some may be tempted to invest in the hottest trend of the day. All too many portfolios have been ruined by this get-rich-quick mentality. In the late 1990s it was tech stocks, a decade ago it was housing in the United States, and in the 17th Century it was tulips in the Netherlands. Now the hottest crazes of the day are marijuana stocks and bitcoin. Money has been made in all of these cases, but the average investor often ends up the biggest loser. If you are hearing about an investment opportunity in the news or from a friend, odds are you are already too late.

So, investing passively is boring and inefficient, and investing in the latest craze is too risky. So, what should the Canadian investor do? Thankfully, there is a middle ground that is both relatively safe and high performing. I have developed a portfolio designed to get the best out of our market, using a logical approach with proper diversification and quality companies. This specific strategy has crushed the overall market in outperformance, growing over 13% per annum since 2011 in a relatively flat period for the Canadian market.

This strategy is available to you today, right here in this book. And I won't even tease it until the last few pages, but instead unveil it in the very next chapter! After that, I will explain why it works, look at how it can fit into a larger investment philosophy, and finally describe the logistics in setting up this strategy yourself so you do not have to pay someone to do so. I hope you are excited and ready to be introduced to what has come to be known as the 6-Pack Portfolio.

CHAPTER 1
THE 6-PACK PORTFOLIO

Picture an investment portfolio as a rock solid 6-pack of abdominal muscles, carefully sculpted and refined through hard work and dedication, giving its owner good looks and athletic performance. Or picture an investment portfolio as a 6-pack of your favourite beverage, helping you to relax after work and enjoy your time off and eventually your retirement. Whatever allegory works best for you, I want the 6-Pack Portfolio to stick in your mind as a concept that makes your money work hard for you and give you peace of mind.

So aside from some fancy metaphors, what exactly is the 6-Pack Portfolio? Its constituents have changed over time, but the basic philosophy has remained the same. Its overall performance has been exceptional in the past, and I still believe it is the best way to invest in the Canadian market. And now, here are the holdings:

The concept for the 6-Pack Portfolio is an equal-weight selection of six stocks in the following industries – Banking, Railroad, Telecommunication, Utility, Pipeline, and Real Estate.

For example, what an investor with $60,000 who subscribes to this philosophy would do is purchase $10,000 worth each of a Bank, Railroad, Telecom, Utility, Pipeline, and REIT (Real Estate Investment Trust) stock. The result is a portfolio that is more balanced, has higher income, and avoids some of the riskier and poor performing sectors in the Canadian economy. The goals of this portfolio can be summed up into three tenets, all of which should be appealing to any investor:

1. Diversification
2. Capital Appreciation
3. Income (Aggregate Goal of 4%)

Much of the discussion of this book will focus on the positives of these six industries, specific stocks to choose, and how they work well together in a portfolio. Before getting into those details, it is useful to know what you are missing out on if you go with this approach rather than just buying a TSX index fund. Take a look at a breakdown of the TSX Composite versus the 6-Pack Portfolio:

Sector Breakdown

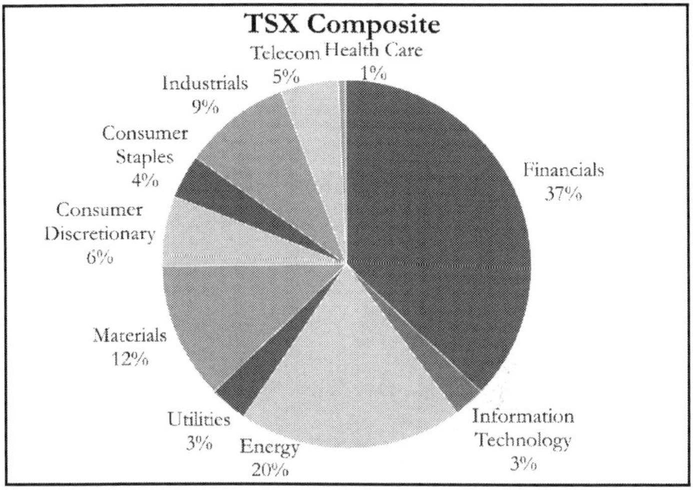

Source: TMXmoney

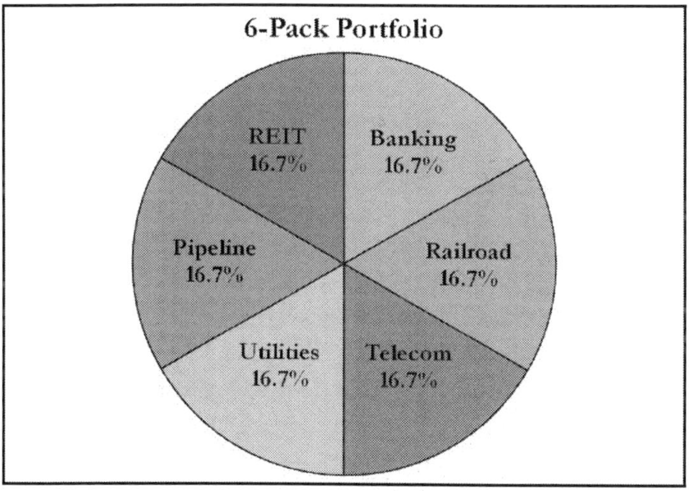

Note that for comparison and clarification, banking stocks make up the majority of the weight in the Financials sector, with life insurance companies and REITs making up a smaller portion. Railroads fall under the Industrials sector, with pipelines fitting into the Energy sector. I will quickly note down a few conclusions you can gather by comparing these pie charts, because the comparison between the TSX Composite and the 6-Pack Portfolio is at the very foundation of our goal of beating the Canadian stock market in Canada.

1. The 6-Pack Portfolio does not have any Materials, Technology, Health Care, or Consumer stocks.
2. The 6-Pack Portfolio is underweight the Financials and Energy sectors.
3. The 6-Pack Portfolio is overweight Railroads, Telecommunications, and Utilities.

Sectors to Avoid

Investing in Canada is as much a question of what not to choose, as it is of what to choose. The Materials, Technology, Health Care, and Consumer stocks in Canada have been completely avoided in the composition of the 6-Pack Portfolio. Why is this the case? My reasoning comes down to a combination of lack of quality, lack of income, and availability of alternatives.

The Materials sector in particular makes up a fairly large portion of the Canadian economy. These stocks are the miners, and in Canada the majority of these names tend to be gold miners that operate internationally in locations around the world. I can say with some confidence that mining stocks are all-around terrible investments, and they will not be missed when you construct a portfolio without representation from this sector. I will go into this line of thinking in more detail in the later section on Gold, but for now I will leave you with this logical thought – is a company a sound investment when it continually depletes its own source of cash flow?

The Technology and Health Care sectors share some characteristics in why they are difficult to recommend as individual names in Canada. For one, these areas are generally difficult to understand unless you are an insider in the industry. I am an advocate of keeping things simple when it comes to investment, and if you do not understand what you are buying then it is almost like becoming a willfully ignorant owner of a company.

For example, Valeant Pharmaceuticals (VRX) was once the darling of the Canadian stock market, even briefly passing Royal Bank (RY) as the largest company by market capitalization in the country. In the last 10 years it went from $18/share in 2007, all the way up to $335 in 2015, only to come crashing back down to $18 again in 2017. That's a 95% loss in value from peak to trough! This is not the kind of volatility you need in a proper portfolio. Unless you were an expert on the health care industry, or correctly identified that Valeant's business model of buying up companies and increasing the price of their drugs was unsustainable, then this could have caused you to lose a ton of money. Owners of TSX Composite index funds of course did lose money, given that Valeant had become such a big name in the overall market.

Another reason not to choose technology or health care names in Canada is that they have better representation south of the border. The global technology industry is dominated by American companies like those represented in the FANG and FAMG acronyms – Facebook, Apple, Amazon, Netflix, Microsoft, and Google. Success stories in Canada have been fleeting – Blackberry comes to mind, which has also lost 95% of its value since its peak in June 2008. Health Care is more of a for-profit industry in the United States, and they have big names like Johnson & Johnson, Pfizer, and Merck available.

The last segment of the Canadian market that is avoided by the 6-Pack Portfolio is the consumer segment, represented by both Consumer Staples and Consumer Discretionary. Some of these stocks have actually performed quite well in recent years, such as Alimentation Couche-Tard (ATD.B) and Dollarama (DOL).

There are two main reasons for avoiding consumer stocks. One is their low dividend yield, which does not align with the income tenet for our portfolio. Another is more of a logical forward-looking conclusion brought about by changing times. It is hard to argue against the fact that more and more shopping will done online, as Amazon continues to grow into a one-stop-shop. Even a more traditional market like grocery may be disrupted, as Whole Foods has been recently bought out and had its prices cut by Amazon. All in all, I believe the low margins of the consumer segment will be squeezed even further, and these stocks will suffer in kind.

The preceding section of this book provides some justification for excluding certain elements of the index from your Canadian portfolio, but that's not the fun part! Next, we will look at in detail, each of the sectors represented by the 6-Pack Portfolio, and the stocks you can pick within them.

Banking

The Canadian stock market is well-known for the prominence of its big banks. The three largest companies in Canada by market capitalization – Royal Bank (RY), TD Bank (TD), and Bank of Nova Scotia (BNS) – highlight the Big 5 Banks, which also includes Bank of Montreal (BMO) and CIBC (CM). The banking sector in Canada is one of the safest in the world, consistently being ranked by the World Economic Forum as top or near-top on its list.

Although they dominate the TSX, making up most of the 37% Financials sector, the 6-Pack Portfolio is comparatively lighter on banking with its one-sixth allocation. This more equal approach to diversification would help in the event of another financial crisis. Admittedly, another stock market crash as in 2008 would likely bring down all stocks, not just the financials. But in the long-run, more equal weight diversification will smooth out returns and help during periods when financials underperform other sectors, such as in 2010 to 2013 when the banks were fairly flat.

But it certainly isn't all bad news with the banks, and owning at least one is a staple of any Canadian portfolio. The banking sector hits on the tenets of the 6-Pack portfolio, providing capital appreciation and dividend yields around the 4% mark. The banks also have a knack of raising their dividends as well, a key consideration for income investors. For example, TD Bank has raised its dividend from 38 cents per share at the start of 2013 to 60 cents in 2017. That is a 73% increase in just 4 years! Given that we know it is a good idea to own a bank stock, the question then becomes which one to choose? As we can see from this chart, they tend to correlate closely with each other:

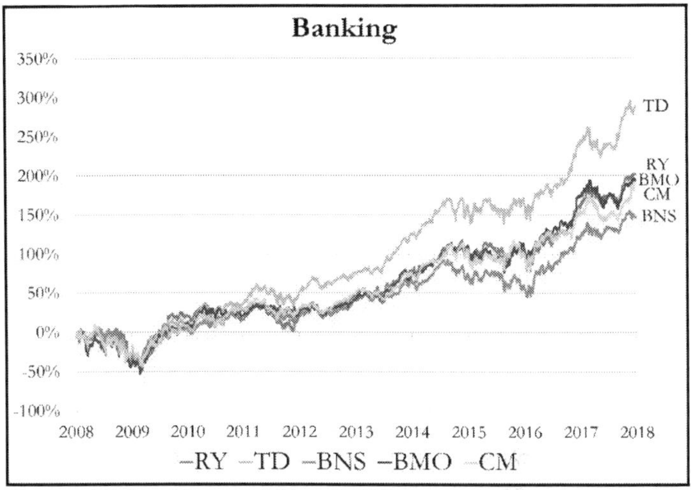

Source: Yahoo Finance Historical Data

If you are reading this book in black and white print, then you will not easily be able to tell the bank colours apart on this chart. That isn't so important, as the intent is to show just how closely the bank stocks follow each other. It makes sense, because events that affect the whole industry, such as interest rates, regulations, and market trends will influence the Big 5 at the same time. Individually, during different time periods some banks will outperform others and vice versa at other times.

As for which stock fits into your portfolio, this comes to personal preference. One method is to choose the bank with whom you do business, that way you will not feel quite so bad about paying your mortgage, bank fees, or stock trading commissions. I tend to view investing from a logical, macroeconomic viewpoint so my own analysis will have that sort of style to it. The banks have the same core business, with the Canadian retail market making up a large portion of their revenue. Taking in deposits, and then lending that money tenfold to the next customer at a higher interest rate is their bread and butter. However, they do have some defining features or identities that can be helpful in deciding which one to choose.

Royal Bank is the market leader and gets business from a variety of sources, including capital markets and internationally. TD Bank has the largest foothold down south, actually becoming one of the ten biggest banks in the USA in its own right. TD also used to be seen as the best customer service bank, but has sort of lost its way with Royal Bank winning the JD Power award in recent years.

Bank of Nova Scotia is the most internationally focused bank; 37% of its revenue (and growing) comes from international banking, compared to 46% from Canadian banking.[1] BMO has done a decent job adapting to changes in the investing environment, offering a suite of ETFs and the first bank owned robo-advisor. CIBC does not really have an identity that comes to mind, and its performance has lagged behind its peers at times. It is easily the worst of the 5 Big Banks and should not be purchased.

In this category, I would recommend holding either Royal Bank, TD Bank, or Scotiabank as part of the 6-Pack Portfolio.

---

[1] Source: PwC 2017 Canadian Banks report

Railroad

Equally as Canadian, and just as long lasting as the banking sector is the railroad industry. Except instead of five, there are just two big railroads on the TSX: Canadian National Railway (CNR) and Canadian Pacific Railway (CP). CN Rail has its headquarters in Montreal and was founded in 1918, while CP Rail is headquartered in Calgary and was incorporated in 1881, becoming the first transcontinental railway in Canada.

There is something romantic about connecting the Atlantic and Pacific Oceans, as it taps into the North American ethos itself. But not just meant for nostalgia, railroads are fantastic investments today! The simplistic difference between these two companies is that CN Rail is more north-south focused while CP Rail is more east-west focused, illustrated by these rail diagrams:

CN Rail System

CP Rail System

Source: Wikipedia

As we can see from the diagrams, CN Rail has an

extensive network that runs as high as the Northwest Territories and down the Mississippi Region into New Orleans. It is well-diversified, with cargo running domestically in Canada and the USA, as well as to various ports for shipment overseas. CP Rail is more cross-country focused, with a lot of its business being commodity shipments to the Pacific Rim through Vancouver. Why is this such a great industry to invest in? The simple answer is that there are not any new railroads. The barriers to entry are so high, that the railroad duopoly in Canada is a safe bet to stay around for the foreseeable future.

The most common benchmark for railroad industry performance is the operating ratio, which measures operating costs as a percentage of revenue (a lower number is better). CN Rail has consistently held low operating ratios (now around 56%), holding the title as the best run railroad in North America. CP Rail historically had very poor operating ratios, but former CN Rail CEO Hunter Harrison turned around the company from 2012 to 2017, dropping the operating ratio from the mid-80s to the high-50s, a staggering increase in efficiency. That efficiency increase was met with a similar stock price increase, as CP jumped from $75/share to $240 in just over two years. In the meantime, CN Rail's stock price has moved ever upward with less volatility. Think of it as a train lumbering steadily up an incline.

Which railroad stock do I ultimately recommend for the 6-Pack Portfolio? The answer is CN Rail, and it is the only stock that has consistently stayed in my own personal portfolio since I started investing. It beats CP because it is a better company and a better stock. I believe the Hunter Harrison era at CP was a one-time efficiency boost that has already played itself out, and CN Rail is the better long-term bet. CNR also has the better dividend yield, coming in at just under 2%. Although that means it is nominally the lowest yielder in the 6-Pack, its dividend growth is nothing short of fantastic, nearly quadrupling in the last 10 years. That infers that the dividend growth has also been accompanied by healthy capital appreciation, as it has over time been the best performer in the 6-Pack Portfolio.

I simply believe that CN Rail is the very best stock in Canada. Bill Gates, founder of Microsoft and one of the world's wealthiest people, agrees with this notion as the largest single shareholder of CNR stock. It should be your portfolio too.

Telecommunication

Another staple industry for investment in Canada is telecommunications. The major players here are Bell (BCE), Telus (T), Rogers (RCI.B), and Shaw (SJR.B). The telecom industry in Canada can trace its roots all the way back to telephone inventor Alexander Graham Bell, who did a lot of his experimentation in our country and is obviously the namesake of Bell Canada. The Rogers family were also pioneers in radio technology. Another old industry dominated by a few companies, are you starting to see a pattern here? Telecom has all of the tools necessary to produce a great stock for your portfolio.

Up until the recent generation, telecommunications only really consisted of the landline telephone and/or television business. Thankfully for investors, the major telecom companies have adapted to the changing times and now operate in the internet/data and wireless industries. Smartphones in particular have been a boon for the telecoms, as Canadians have no qualms about spending ~$75/month on their phone bills. The industry is governed by the Canadian Radio-television and Telecommunications Commission (CRTC), which in short provides both regulation and protection to these companies. Here is a look at CRTC data for the telecom industry in Canada:

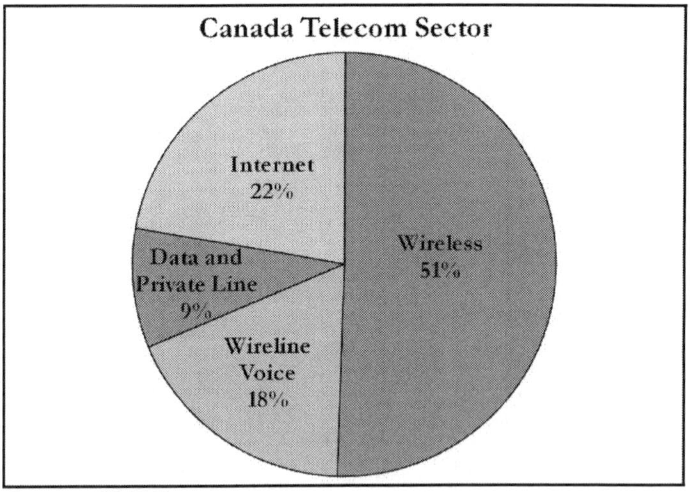

Source: CRTC

So which telecom is the best choice for the 6-Pack Portfolio? Correlations between the four major players is high, just like with the banks. I would immediately discount Shaw, as they do not have near as much as a mobility presence through their Freedom Mobile subsidiary as the big three. Wireless market share in Canada is split fairly evenly between Bell, Telus, and Rogers, with smaller players making up only about 10% total.

Defining features between these three companies are along two subjects: geographic and unique lines of business. Geographically, Telus is the major provider in Western Canada – British Columbia and Alberta especially, while Bell is the dominant player in Eastern Canada – Ontario, Quebec, the Atlantic, and Manitoba following the purchase of Manitoba Telecom. Rogers has a presence across Canada, but is more concentrated in Ontario. Bell and Rogers also both hold significant media and entertainment assets, having a joint share in Maple Leafs Sports & Entertainment – owners of the Toronto Maple Leafs, Toronto Raptors, and Toronto FC. Rogers also owns the Blue Jays baseball team, as well as the Sportsnet series of channels. Bell has a stake in the Montreal Canadiens as well as being the owner of various television channels such as CTV and TSN.

My favourite telecom in Canada and my choice for the 6-Pack Portfolio would have to be Telus. It helps that it is my provider for services, so I do not feel as bad paying my phone bill when I am also collecting dividends from the company. I also feel it is more of a pure play on telecommunications, as they are not caught up in the business of old media like television content and sports entertainment that perhaps is not the place for a lot of growth.

As far as their own side businesses, Telus is starting to focus more on the health industry with Telus Health, which is likely a good bet with an aging population in Canada. I also think that Western Canada is probably a better place growth-wise, despite the current low oil prices in Alberta. Telus and Bell both have good dividend policies, with decent yields above 4% and annual or bi-annual increases. For that reason, I would rank them in this order – Telus, Bell, Rogers, and Shaw.

Utilities

There is perhaps no sector in the stock market more boring than utilities. Even when playing Monopoly, the thought of landing on an unowned utility fails to generate much excitement. So, are the utilities on the TSX worth buying? Given that the industry takes a place in the 6-Pack Portfolio, I would of course say yes. A utility in your portfolio will lower your overall volatility, provide some consistent dividends, and hold its value better than more cyclical stocks during a potential recession. No matter the scenario, everybody still needs to pay their gas and electric bill!

There is a bit more variety in stock choices for utility companies in Canada than the railroad and telecommunications industries. There is also some similarity and business overlap with pipelines, another 6-Pack sector. Some of the smaller utilities should be avoided, either because of poor performance (TA: TransAlta) or because their business is essentially door-to-door sales (JE: Just Energy). So, what we are looking for in a utility is a steady cash flow from regulated and non-regulated grid-like assets, usually natural gas and electricity. The names I will focus on the TSX are Fortis (FTS), Emera (EMA), Canadian Utilities (CU), and Algonquin Power & Utilities (AQN).

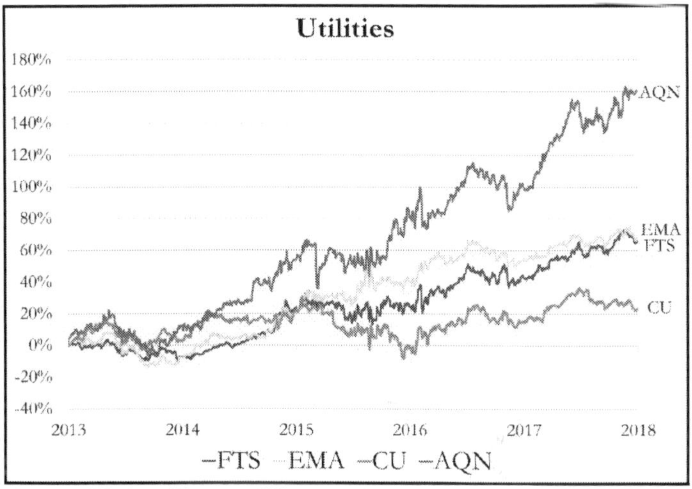

Source: Yahoo Finance Historical Data

Fortis and Canadian Utilities are the kings of dividend growth history not only in the utility space, but when compared to the entire TSX. With streaks of 43 and 45 years respectively, FTS and CU have raised their dividend every year since the 1970s, rewarding long-term shareholders with a reliable income stream that beats inflation. That record is nearly double any near competitors.

Fortis is based in Newfoundland, but has expanded throughout Canada, the USA, and the Caribbean with mostly regulated electricity and natural gas service. Canadian Utilities is based in Alberta, and is a subsidiary of ATCO (ACO.X). It takes some digging to find out how this relationship works and how much of the ATCO umbrella you are getting when you purchase CU, but the conglomerate as a whole has expanded throughout Canada and internationally into the USA, Mexico, Europe, and Australia.

Emera and Algonquin Power & Utilities have a healthy dividend yield of around 4.5%, roughly a full percentage point higher than FTS and CU. Both EMA and AQN have raised their dividends regularly, with AQN in particular having impressive growth – its stock price has tripled and its dividend has doubled since 2010. Note that Algonquin pays its dividends in USD, so consider holding its NYSE equivalent in an account where you need American money for other purchases.

Emera and Algonquin have a shorter history, being listed on the TSX in the late 1990s. Emera is based in Nova Scotia and has holdings throughout the United States and the Caribbean, while Algonquin is based in Ontario and has holdings all over North America. Algonquin also has a higher focus on water services than the other utilities on our list, and also has investments in clean energy with wind, solar, and thermal power assets.

As for which utility stock I recommend for

placement in the 6-Pack Portfolio, it would be hard to go wrong with any of these four. For a size comparison, Fortis has a market capitalization of ~$17.5 billion, with Canadian Utilities and Emera at ~$10 billion and Algonquin Power & Utilities at ~$5 billion. If you want the long-term history of performance and dividend increases at a lower yield, my pick would be Fortis. For some growth and diversity in the utility sector at a higher yield, Algonquin is an interesting choice. Perhaps utilities aren't so boring after all?

Pipeline

The pipeline business is perhaps the most tenuous sector in the 6-Pack Portfolio right now. The price of oil has taken a beating since 2014, with only a modest recovery since the lows of 2016. There are clouds over the oil industry in general, with oversupply and a threatened shift to more cleaner sources of energy in the future. Pipelines also face continuous opposition for approval of new projects, as they get stuck in bureaucracy with politicians afraid to commit and with protests from environmentalists.

Looking back at our 6-Pack tenets, pipelines are great for dividend yield and as a way to access the energy sector for diversification. But perhaps they are not the best choice for future-proofing. However, the one-sixth allocation to pipelines is still less than the 20% exposure to the Energy sector you would be getting when buying the TSX index. It also is focused on just that – pipelines, and not the more volatile energy extraction business. I still think a pipeline has a place in your portfolio, and it could even be a bargain at today's prices.

Notable pipelines listed on the TSX include: Enbridge (ENB), TransCanada (TRP), Inter Pipeline (IPL), Pembina Pipeline (PPL), and Enbridge Income Fund (ENF). After Enbridge's merger with Spectra Energy in February 2017, it is now a massive company with a ~$75 billion market capitalization – one of the five largest stocks in Canada and the biggest energy infrastructure company in North America. TransCanada is also a continent-wide large cap company with ~$50 billion in value. Pembina and Inter Pipeline are mid-sized and more regionally focused in the Alberta area, with the latter also having natural gas storage in Europe.

As mentioned previously, the most significant issue for these pipelines in growing their business is the current political climate and the approval, or lack thereof, of new projects. Enbridge's Northern Gateway has been shelved, and TransCanada's Keystone XL and Energy East projects are still caught up in the investment-unfriendly world of protests and regulation. A lot of the protesting over singular pipeline projects may be seen as ironic, considering the current map of pipelines on the continent:

Pipelines in North America

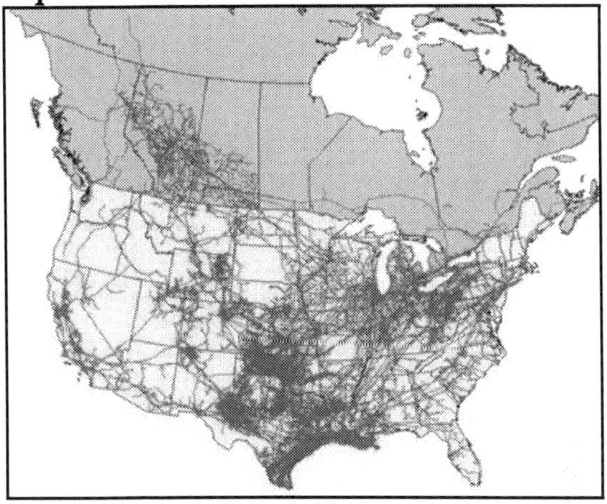

Source: Globe and Mail (February 19, 2011)

Clearly pipelines are not a new thing, and the demand for oil and natural gas in a modern economy will facilitate its arrival in another fashion if new projects are forever held up. Oil can and does come from railways, which is a less safe transport method than in pipelines. It also comes in tankers overseas from governments with questionable morals like Venezuela and Saudi Arabia. Admittedly, pipeline opposition may base itself on hoping for a greener world in general, and therefore any logical pro-pipeline arguments will not win their side over. So, I suspect the new pipeline quagmire will continue. An investor alone cannot change the state of the world, and should invest accordingly.

That is why I hold and recommend Enbridge Income Fund (ENF) for the pipeline component in the 6-Pack Portfolio. It holds mature Enbridge pipelines as assets, and is designed to provide its investors with cash flow as monthly distributions. Normally mature operations with less of a focus on growth can be a downside to investment, but in the pipeline world I consider that aspect a benefit of Enbridge Income Fund. ENF has an attractive ~8% dividend yield, which boosts the aggregate yield of the 6-Pack, and has also performed just as well or better than the parent ENB stock price in the past few years. Although pipelines have been a tough business to be in since 2014, I would continue to hold ENF for its yield and as a way to access a potential rebound in the energy sector.

REIT

Real Estate Investment Trusts, or REITs as they are commonly known, are a unique addition to the 6-Pack Portfolio. Many investors choose to assemble a portfolio with real estate as its own allocation, whether it be via physical property, REITs, or other investment vehicles. I tend to view REITs as a different, but related investment to real estate. The 6-Pack thinking is that REITs behave like a stock, and can function as a specific part of your stock portfolio.

One option that investors can undertake to maintain a real estate allocation is to buy the XRE ETF on the TSX, which gives you access to a variety of REITs in Canada in one holding. The problem with this approach is that XRE has a ludicrous expense ratio of 0.61%, meaning you'll effectively be giving iShares about 12% of your dividend yield just for the privilege of owning their easily replicable product. Real estate securities are an area where it definitely makes sense to buy your own stocks.

So, what are the options an investor has when choosing a REIT for his or her portfolio? With the other 6-Pack categories, there is a tendency that each company provides essentially the same service – the difference between BMO and CIBC is quite subtle, and the consumer will likely find very similar products at each bank. With REITs, there is not a homogenous approach to their business, as different companies will focus on residential, commercial, industrial, or office properties. Some have a further defined focus, for instance Chartwell Retirement Residences (CSH.UN) holds retirement housing for seniors, which could be an interesting play on shifting demographics in Canada.

More than any other 6-Pack category, REITs require some simple and logical analysis that can be crucial for your portfolio performance. For instance, a switch from the largest REIT in Canada, RioCan (REI.UN) to Canadian Apartment Properties (CAR.UN) in the summer of 2016 has since benefited my own REIT allocation's performance by 25%. You can see below that these REITs had some correlation in the past, but in the last few years RioCan has really lagged behind.

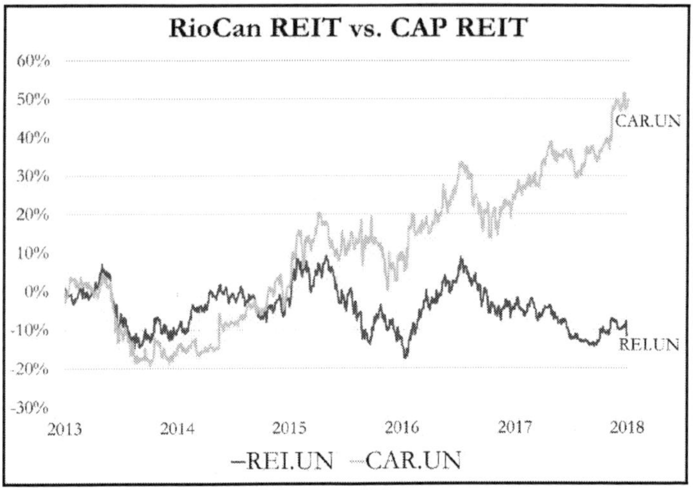

Source: Yahoo Finance Historical Data

What is the reasoning behind both my switch, and the subsequent stock price divergence? The simple answer is the death of retail shopping, both perceived and real. A lot of REITs, including RioCan, have most of their assets and square footage in retail shopping malls. Although retail will not be completely replaced by online shopping, it is in an obvious downward trend, and that sort of investment should always be avoided. The stock market is forward-looking, and even though some of the REITs in retail may still have good financial numbers, in the future they will find that their big-name tenants will start to dry-up. For example, as I write this chapter, Toys-R-Us in the USA has declared bankruptcy and I am sure other big retail names will follow.

There are too many different REITs on the TSX to list here, but hopefully you have more of an idea on how to analyze what holding could be the best for your portfolio. I recommend Canadian Apartment Properties (CAP REIT), the stock I switched to from RioCan, as my top pick. CAP REIT has over 50,000 residential units across Canada, and they are not tied to any one location – their holdings are coast to coast. People will always need a place to live, and given the rising cost of housing I think apartments will be a great investment for the foreseeable future.

I will talk more about 6-Pack expansion in the next section, but keep in mind for now one interesting method would be to split your REIT allocation in half between CAR.UN and Canadian REIT (REF.UN). The latter is more of a classic REIT, with square footage diversified between retail, industrial, and office across Canada. But it rewards investors more than something like RioCan, with REF.UN offering regular annual distribution increases and a solid reputation for management. Between the two securities you would have a good mix of all types of real estate, and a ~4% distribution yield set to grow annually.

However, the best part about owning a REIT is that you have the benefit of being a landlord with none of the extra work. You don't have to worry about plumbing, renovations, or bad tenants. The experienced and professional teams at these companies will take care of it for you, while you can kick back and enjoy your 6-Pack.

Bottom Line

- The 6-Pack Portfolio consists of Bank, Railroad, Telecom, Utility, Pipeline, and REIT stocks in equal weights.
- It avoids or discounts the Materials, Energy, Consumer, Technology, and Health Care sectors in order to focus on what works best in the Canadian market.
- The 6-Pack Portfolio is designed to give you diversification, capital appreciation, and income that is superior to investing in the TSX Composite Index.

12-Pack Portfolio

Now that we've taken a look at all of the sectors in the 6-Pack Portfolio, perhaps you are wanting a bit more. Is the 6-Pack Portfolio not enough to quench your thirst? You can try doubling the 6-Pack to create your very own 12-Pack Portfolio.

In all seriousness, this can be a viable option for many people. If you're at the stage in your life where you have a lot of money, your 6-stock set can be expanded in order to diversify a bit more. I would say that if your Canadian stock allocation calls for an investment above $100,000, you can safely split that money up among 12 stocks. You would still stick to the principles of the 6-Pack Portfolio, but add an additional stock from each sector. For example, hold both Telus and BCE in equal parts for your telecom allocation.

This method won't necessarily increase performance over the 6-Pack, but it will reduce specific company risk. You are now less exposed to any one event impacting your portfolio too much, like a major spill at a pipeline or bad press for one of the banks or telecoms. In my backtesting of the 6-Pack Portfolio, which is covered in the next chapter, having pairs of stocks in equal weight in each of the six sectors did decrease deviation of returns. A decreased standard deviation of returns translates into lower risk for the portfolio overall.

One caveat I would give if you decide to go with 12 stocks is that CP Rail does not necessarily provide the best compliment to the overall portfolio. And there's really only two options when it comes to railroads – CN Rail and CP Rail. CP struggles a bit to pull its weight when considering the income tenet of the 6-Pack, as it only has a 1% dividend yield. You can alleviate this pressure by not including CP Rail, or by decreasing its weight relative to CNR. Here is a possible portfolio allocation if you decide to go with the 12-Pack:

Name	Symbol	Sector	Weight
TD Bank	TD	Bank	10.00%
Scotiabank	BNS	Bank	10.00%
CN Rail	CNR	Railroad	10.00%
CP Rail	CP	Railroad	6.00%
Telus	T	Telecom	8.00%
BCE	BCE	Telecom	8.00%
Fortis	FTS	Utility	8.00%
Emera	EMA	Utility	8.00%
ENB Income Fund	ENF	Pipeline	8.00%
Inter Pipeline	IPL	Pipeline	8.00%
CAP REIT	CAR.UN	REIT	8.00%
Canadian REIT	REF.UN	REIT	8.00%

The above portfolio is almost equal weight between the sectors, with the banks having a slightly higher allocation. Functionally, it will be almost the same as the 6-Pack Portfolio, but with less specific company risk. The downside is that the performance may lag a bit if your second choice in a sector is not as good as the first, and that you must keep track of more companies and pay more trading commissions.

A note on stock trading commissions: this is

something we haven't talked about much yet. But if you're a beginning investor, you should know that for every trade, your stock brokerage will take a commission. For the big banks, this is usually $10. This is why when you are starting out with smaller amounts of money, it wouldn't be a good idea to hold the 12-Pack Portfolio, because you would be paying too much in commissions to buy and sell your holdings. Later on, when you have a 6-figure portfolio, the $10 trades won't mean much relatively.

Bottom Line

- You can expand the 6-Pack Portfolio to include 12 stocks in order to reduce specific company risk, choosing an additional name in each sector.
- Consider choosing this method if your Canadian stock allocation calls for more than $100,000.
- Exclude or reduce the allocation of CP Rail to keep a higher aggregate income for your portfolio.

CHAPTER 2
PERFORMANCE

"An ounce of performance is worth pounds of promises."
– Mae West

This book is about beating the Canadian stock market, so I better provide some proof that the 6-Pack Portfolio has actually done so. And it has. Every year since inception, the 6-Pack has performed better than the TSX Composite Index. I personally bought the initial holdings in 2011, and have maintained them in every calendar year up until the end of 2017. The last seven years is a decent sample size in an investing time horizon, at least enough to discount the probability that the 6-Pack Portfolio's success is due to luck. I don't guarantee outperformance every year going forward, but the results have certainly been impressive so far.

Performance vs. Benchmark

Year	6-Pack	TSX	Alpha
2011	15.35%	-8.71%	24.06%
2012	17.74%	7.19%	10.55%
2013	15.32%	12.99%	2.33%
2014	22.66%	10.55%	12.11%
2015	-5.87%	-8.32%	2.45%
2016	24.10%	21.08%	3.02%
2017	10.18%	9.10%	1.08%
Overall	13.80%	5.76%	8.04%

The above data represents the time-weighted rate of returns of both the 6-Pack Portfolio and the TSX Composite. Note that the TSX returns include dividends on the plus side, but don't include anything like trading commissions or cash-drag on the negative side that you would expect to find in a real-life portfolio. The 6-Pack returns are my actual performance numbers within my brokerage account, so they include all the 'real-world' aspects. Cash-drag means the uninvested cash within your portfolio that counts towards your performance numbers, but will not add to your performance.

Time-weighted returns are the best way to calculate the theoretical growth of an initial investment over time. As we can see from the table, the 6-Pack has been consistently better than the TSX Composite over the last seven years, including some really substantial outperformance in 2011, 2012, and 2014. Over time this has added up to an 8% annual alpha, meaning an aggregate 8% performance above the benchmark. These performance figures are something that most "money-managers" could never aspire to. What does that mean in dollar figures? Let's examine the theoretical growth of $10,000 over seven years:

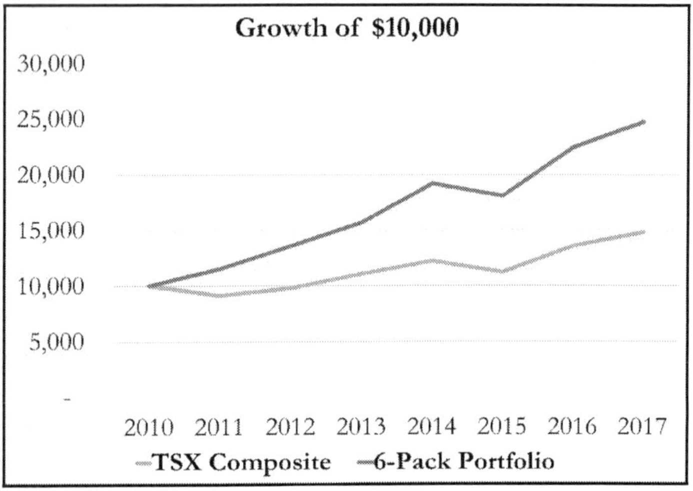

For the hypothetical investor who put $10,000 into the TSX Composite Index seven years ago, it would have grown to $14,803. Investing in the 6-Pack Portfolio by comparison turned $10,000 into $24,725. The difference itself was an astounding $10,000 over 7 years, the entire amount of the initial investment! If you stretch this kind of outperformance out over 30 years, that difference could be millions. Naturally, I don't anticipate 8% alpha indefinitely, and would be happy with 2-3% above the benchmark index over a long period of time.

A question that seasoned investors may ask is whether the outperformance of the 6-Pack Portfolio has come as the result of taking on more risk. I always look for opportunities with low risk and high reward, even though the traditional investment thinking states: to get more reward you need to take more risk. But if you take perhaps the most common measure of risk, standard deviation, the 6-Pack Portfolio actually has lower risk than the TSX Composite.

Using the preceding table figures as data, the last seven years gives the TSX a standard deviation of returns of 10.20%, while the 6-Pack has a standard deviation of 9.29%. Basically, the TSX Index has deviated more from its average return than the 6-Pack, thus being more unpredictable and risky. And this is despite the index having ~1500 stocks as opposed to just 6. If you were to use the 12-Pack Portfolio variant, you would have even less standard deviation. The holdings we have chosen are less volatile, especially considering we have left out some cyclical names such as mining and resource stocks.

Remember that the 6-Pack Portfolio is made up of stocks and is therefore risky by nature, so don't expect the outsized returns of the past to continue indefinitely. We have been lucky since 2009 to have participated in a bull market. But there are signs that the 6-Pack Portfolio will do well in a bear market too. 2015 was its only down year so far, largely due to the terrible performance of its pipeline component when oil prices sunk. But the TSX fared even worse, thanks to its oversized Energy allocation. And 2011 was also a poor year for the Canadian stock market, but the 6-Pack managed to crush the index by 24%.

Hypothetical Backtesting

Seven years may not be a long enough timeframe and sample size for some people to be convinced about the viability of the 6-Pack Portfolio. So, I ran some backtesting since the year 2000 with the data available on the handy website: www.portfoliovisualizer.com. The 6-Pack stocks I used for the benchmark comparison were TD Bank (TD), CN Rail (CNR), Telus (T), Fortis (FTS), Enbridge (ENB), and Canadian REIT (REF.UN). I used XIU for the benchmark, which covers the S&P TSX 60 Index, because it has a long history. It has more of a large cap focus than the general index, but its performance numbers mirror the broader XIC very closely. The results:

Category	6-Pack	TSX 60
Initial Balance	$10,000	$10,000
Final Balance	$123,917	$30,425
CAGR*	15.01%	6.38%
Stdev	10.50%	13.89%
Best Year	32.28%	31.31%
Worst Year	-14.49%	-31.09%

**CAGR: Compound Annual Growth Rate, an annualized measure of performance.*

As you can see, the 6-Pack Portfolio has vastly outperformed the general Canadian stock market since the turn of the century. Starting in the January 2000 with $10,000, an investment into the TSX 60 has grown to $30,425 at the end of December 2017.

The 6-Pack Portfolio has grown that same $10,000 to a whopping $123,917, at an amazing 15% compound annual growth rate.

Not only has the 6-Pack had better performance, but it has done so with less risk as measured by standard deviation. Its worst year in 2008 was only half as bad as the index too. The only year that the TSX showed notable outperformance over the 6-Pack was in 2007, during the commodity boom. I believe that the only real scenario where the 6-Pack would lag the index is in a prolonged commodity bull market, because our stock picks lack miners and drillers of resources. But commodities are cyclical by nature, and the companies themselves are chasing after ever-depleting resources.

Keep in mind that this is all hypothetical backtesting. I tend to value the real-world data of my own account since 2011 higher, because money was on the line and it was forward-looking at the time. Unfortunately, you cannot go back in time and order that juicy 15% annual performance. Backtesting these names also lends itself to survivorship bias, whereby the names that are prevalent today had a higher chance of surviving and performing well in the past.

The point of the backtesting since the year 2000 was to provide a higher sample size and timeframe, giving tangible evidence that the 6-Pack Portfolio has beat the performance of the Canadian stock market. Why it works, and whether this past performance can be repeated in the future is the subject of the next chapter.

Bottom Line

- The 6-Pack Portfolio has beat the TSX Composite Index every year since inception in 2011, boasting an 8% performance alpha despite lower risk.
- Compounded annual growth of 13.80% in the past seven years was good enough to grow a theoretical $10,000 to almost $25,000.
- Backtesting to the year 2000 gives similar results, with the 6-Pack Portfolio showing an 8.63% alpha and lower risk.

CHAPTER 3
WHY IT WORKS

Given the great performance figures of the 6-Pack Portfolio since its inception, there is naturally an inclination to explain why it has done so well. Investment performance, especially in the stock market, is not a sure thing. But I believe that the composition of a portfolio can set it up for success, and that some of the reasoning behind the 6-Pack investment philosophy can help explain that success. In this chapter, I will delve more into the theory of the 6-Pack Portfolio.

The stock selection and philosophy did not necessarily follow one another in a certain order, but rather over time they have developed in tandem. What I mean by that is – the 6-Pack stocks weren't picked and then a theory built on top of them, nor was a theory built and then stock selections pigeonholed to fit that theory. Headlined below are the core theories of the portfolio, and the similarities that these types of stocks share with one another. These are characteristics that I believe make the 6-Pack Portfolio successful in the long-run, as they are not necessarily dependent on management success or good ideas – but rather the very nature of the industry.

Oligopoly

The word oligopoly comes from Greek meaning 'few sellers', in contrast to monopoly which of course means only 'one seller'. In practice, this means an industry where market share is dominated by a few major players. I will not go deeply into the economics behind an oligopolistic market, but briefly explain some of the benefits that these companies can enjoy.

Generally, oligopolies are able to set and maintain higher prices, and thus earn higher profit margins. Some organizations do this blatantly, as in the case of cartels like the oil producing OPEC group. In countries like Canada where this sort of behaviour is regulated or illegal, the price collusion is more subtle.

Oligopolies have other characteristics – namely high barriers to entry for the industry, little alternatives available to the consumer, and having a largely similar product to their competitors. Economic theory states that oligopolies can retain economic profits (different than accounting profits) in the long-run, something that most companies cannot do.

You can start to imagine how the 6-Pack Portfolio takes advantage of the benefits of oligopolistic markets. The classic example is the telecommunications industry, where Bell, Telus and Rogers make up over 90% of the cell phone market. This is the tightest telecom oligopoly in the entire developed world, and Canadians are the ones paying for it – with the highest plan rates among all peer countries. Rather than fight against the current scenario, profit from it by owning one of them in your portfolio.

There are some other obvious oligopolies within the 6-Pack framework, that share many of the same characteristics. The Big 5 Banks control the market share for finance in this country, and when one (usually Royal Bank) sets the price on something like mortgage rates, the others will follow. CN Rail and CP Rail are the only two notable railroads in Canada, and emphasize the longevity and staying power that is evident in both oligopolies and the 6-Pack Portfolio. Pipelines and utilities fill the characteristics of offering a homogenized product and leaving few alternatives for consumers.

REITs are perhaps the only 6-Pack category that does not have clear characteristics of an oligopoly, as there are many real estate companies to choose from on the TSX, and they can offer a variety of services – apartments, shopping malls, industrial, health care, etc. However, REITs still offer other attractive benefits that strengthen the 6-Pack Portfolio as a whole.

Infrastructure

Related to oligopolies, infrastructure in place is a key component of why I believe 6-Pack industries perform well as investments. Having large scale infrastructure in place is a reason why some of these companies have thrived for over a century with little threat of direct competition.

For example, the railroad network in Canada is generations old and mostly owned by the two big names – CN Rail and CP Rail. The likelihood of a railroad company in the 21st Century starting up and laying its tracks in a large country like Canada is near zero. The same benefits apply to pipelines, utilities, and telecoms. Pipes in the ground, electric and natural gas grids, wireless towers and data cables, it's all simple to conceptualize. This sort of capital investment is difficult to undertake upfront, so with the infrastructure already in place these companies have a distinct advantage – and can perform maintenance on or modernize their grids over time.

To go along with the notion that companies in these oligopoly-type industries subtly work together, often this infrastructure is shared between the firms. For example, railroads will use each other's tracks, pipelines will connect with each other, and telecoms will piggyback off each other's wireless towers and data cables. In a word, it's all one big *network* with a high barrier to entry for new companies.

Related to infrastructure, oligopolies, and their high barriers to entry is regulation. Many of the 6-

Pack industries, especially utilities and telecoms, are examples of highly regulated businesses. I won't delve too deeply into the topic of regulation, but the CRTC and other regulatory bodies likely decrease the chance of new competitors, and increase the price certainty for the names in their industry.

Dividends

The above categories focus on unique aspects of 6-Pack industries and how that can benefit the underlying stock. That sort of benefit is more conceptual though, and can only be realized over a long timeframe in the success of a company. However, a dividend is cash in your hand every quarter or every month, and the benefits of collecting this cash flow impacts your portfolio returns every year and beyond. If we look back to the tenets of the 6-Pack Portfolio, income at around 4% annually is a goal. All six industries pay dividends, and most have policies or a track record of regularly raising those dividends.

There is much debate in the investment community as to the value of a dividend. The types of investors who swear by totally efficient markets will generally fall into the camp of what I call "dividend denial". Their argument is that a dividend paid to the investor will immediately decrease the value of the company by that amount. For example, if a $40.00 stock pays a dividend of $1.00 per share to its shareholders, then afterwards it is worth $39.00. This argument does hold up in the short run, as you will often see a stock price drop by its dividend value on the ex-dividend date. But in the long-run, collecting dividends from your stocks and reinvesting them will provide you with better portfolio performance.

In fact, the longer you go back, the higher the percentage of your returns will come from reinvested dividends. You can see this through the historical S&P 500 calculator on the Don't Quit Your Day Job website.[2] If the past ~150 years of data is anything to go by, then in a lifetime of investing, reinvested dividends will account for over 90% of your total returns. And that is just on an index, not a portfolio that is specifically designed around dividend-paying companies. Dividends are a reliable and controllable way of taking advantage of the magic of compound interest, something that is out of your hands when it comes to stock price appreciation.

When you think of compound interest, you often think of a steady interest rate that you collect or pay over time; for example, 5% annual interest locked in for 10 years. Generally speaking, this is how it works for bonds, GICs, loans, and mortgages with fixed rates or coupons. What is great about dividend-paying stocks, and what can really supercharge your compounded returns are the dividend growth rates in the 6-Pack Portfolio.

Take for example CN Rail, which is nominally the lowest yielder in the portfolio at under 2% per

---

[2] https://dqydj.com/sp-500-return-calculator

annum. In 2007 it paid a split-adjusted dividend per share of 10.5 cents. Ten years later in 2017 that same dividend is 41.25 cents per share, representing a near quadruple in income! This means that although the initial dividend yield on shares of CNR bought in 2007 was 1.75%, the effective yield on those shares today is nearly 7%.

I am not necessarily a fan of the effective yield approach to evaluating investments, as I believe each asset in your portfolio should be assessed on a current and future basis. But it can be effective in showing just how powerful dividend growth stocks can be, and offers a way to take advantage of compounding in an era when 10-year bonds pay ~2% in interest without any growth.

Furthermore, collecting dividends is a way to actively participate in a company's success throughout its lifetime, especially for long-term buy and hold investors. Many stocks rise and fall, and some disappear altogether. If a stock disappears without ever paying you a dividend, you have nothing tangible to show for having owned that company.

Simplicity

I am a big fan of keeping it simple when investing. That philosophy extends to the companies themselves within a portfolio. A quote attributed to famed investors Warren Buffett and Peter Lynch states that you want to invest in companies that any idiot could run – because someday an idiot will probably run it.

The 6-Pack Portfolio is filled with toll-booth like companies. You drive over the bridge, you pay the toll. The same thing with these stocks, they provide the infrastructure and collect the fees. CAP REIT provides apartments, then collects the rent every month. Telecoms provide the network, then collect the phone and internet bills every month. Banks have all sorts of regular monthly income via account fees, mortgage payments, etc. Railroads, utilities, and pipelines are so simple to think about – send the train down the track, send the electricity down the wire, send the oil down the pipe. Collect the reliable income, then rinse and repeat. It's all very simple!

Bottom Line

- 6-Pack Portfolio industries are characterized as oligopolies, restricting competition and allowing for economic profits in the long run. Their business models are simple, leaving the investor with confidence on what they are putting their money into.
- 6-Pack companies have infrastructure in place that helps maintain their competitive advantage and put up high barriers to entry – i.e. railroads, pipelines, and communications networks.
- The 6-Pack Portfolio is designed around companies that pay a healthy dividend, around 4% in aggregate. Unlike simple interest, these dividends rise over time and provide an excellent source of compounded growth.

CHAPTER 4
ASSET ALLOCATION

In this chapter I will outline how the 6-Pack Portfolio can fit into a broader asset allocation. Remember that the 6-Pack stocks are only companies based in Canada, and can only fit into the equity portion of your portfolio. In order to complement the stock choices we have already made, it is necessary to look at a variety of other assets – US & International Stocks, Bonds, Cash, and Precious Metals.

Why worry about asset allocation? Much like splitting the 6-Pack stocks into six different industries, the idea is to take advantage of diversification. Nobel Prize winner Harry Markowitz called diversification the only free lunch in finance. I will not go heavily into the math and economics behind diversification, but the main idea is to spread your assets into different baskets, preferably ones that have low or negative correlation with each other.

As an example, if there is poor economic news such as an unexpected rise in unemployment, the value of stocks are likely to decrease and the value of bonds are likely to increase. This is what I mean by negative correlation: when one goes down, the other goes up and vice versa. Over time this should result in a smoothing of returns, thereby decreasing your overall risk at no cost to your risk-adjusted returns. Hence the free lunch.

Although I do recommend diversifying your assets outside of Canadian stocks, thankfully this process is very simple – even more simple than the 6-Pack Portfolio. As we have previously talked about, there is a benefit in picking and choosing when it comes to the TSX, as there are some unique aspects of the Canadian stock market that rewards this approach. With other asset classes, there is less of a reason to do so, and that asset can be owned with just a simple index purchase. In the following subsections, I will discuss the other asset classes, and at the end of this chapter will provide some sample allocations that complement the 6-Pack Portfolio.

US Stocks

The United States has the largest and most efficient stock market in the world, with its market capitalization coming in at over 50% of the world's total stock market value. Over the last 100 years the USA has grown to become the leading industrial and financial power, housing many of the world's large international corporations. As of the start of 2018, the top five names on that list are all massive technology companies: Apple, Microsoft, Alphabet (Google), Amazon, and Facebook. Despite the top-heavy weight in tech, the overall mix of sectors in the US market is actually quite balanced, shown on the following graph:

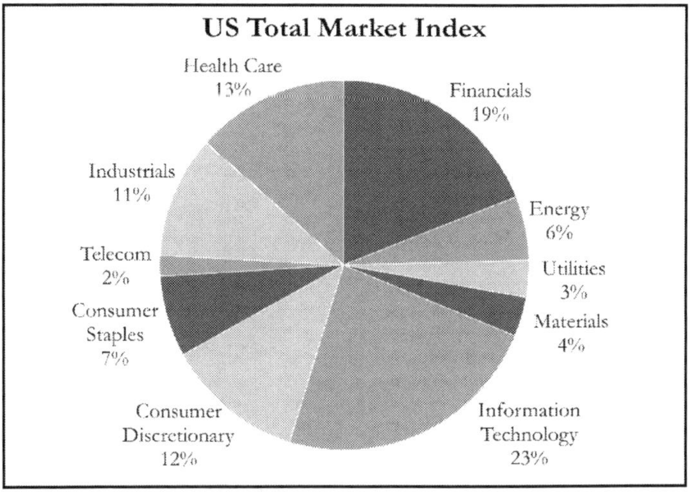

Source: S&P Dow Jones Indices

Key differences between the US and Canadian stock markets include:

1. The US market has a much larger share of Technology and Health Care stocks.
2. The Canadian market has a much larger proportion of Energy and Financial stocks.
3. The US market has a larger share of Consumer Goods & Services stocks.

Recall that the 6-Pack Portfolio does not have any technology, health care, or consumer stock components. Therefore, the US Total Stock Market index is a near perfect complement to the Canadian stocks we have already chosen.

The reasons for choosing an index for exposure to the US stock market are many. First, the US market is widely followed and very efficient, meaning that it is more difficult to design market-beating strategies. Most money managers fail to beat the S&P 500. Second, as a Canadian investor your time and focus for stock selection can stay in your home country rather than following a much larger market down south. And third, the aforementioned health care and technology stocks fit into a category of security that I believe is hard to understand unless you are an industry insider. It is difficult to find the next big technology stock, and owning the index will get you exposure to the industry in general without having to make those tough choices.

So, what is the best way to get access to the American market? You can very easily buy the Total Market Index as outlined in the above graph by purchasing the Vanguard Total Stock Market ETF (VTI) on the New York Stock Exchange. This fund has an expense ratio of just 0.04%, meaning a $10,000 investment would only pay $4 in fees per year. This cost is essentially nothing and will not affect your long-term returns.

Another option is to buy the S&P 500 Index (SPY), which holds 500 companies in the standard benchmark index. The main difference between these funds is that SPY is solely large cap focused, with VTI holding the entire market. In practice, these funds will mirror each other pretty closely as the large caps tend to dominate the makeup and direction of VTI anyways. I would recommend buying VTI, unless you wish to trade options on the underlying stock (not relevant for most people), in which case SPY has the more liquid market.

<u>Bottom Line</u>

- The US stock market is large, diversified, efficient, and very hard to beat for money managers.
- US Stocks are a great complement to the sectors in the 6-Pack Portfolio – you get exposure to quality technology, health care, and consumer stocks.
- Buy the Vanguard Total Stock Market ETF (VTI) for one-stop access to the American market.

International & Emerging Market Stocks

So far, we have only talked about North America, but there is a much wider international stock market to consider. Generally, when we refer to International stocks, we are talking about developed nations such as those in Western Europe, Australia, Japan, and South Korea. Emerging Markets will make up the rest of the world, which includes China, India, and Brazil. But is it worth investing internationally? As we can see from this 10-year chart, performance for global stocks compared to the American market has been woeful:

Source: Yahoo Finance Historical Data

Index performance for International (VEA) and Emerging Market (VWO) stocks has actually been negative in the last 10 years, never fully recovering from the stock market crash of 2008 as of the end of 2017. Of course, it is not entirely wise to assume that the next 10 years will be the same as the last 10 years. Global stocks could outperform in the future. But there are several reasons why I am cautious about recommending them in an investment portfolio:

1. The Total US Stock Market Index already offers a perfect compliment to the 6-Pack Portfolio in terms of sector diversification.
2. Global stock market correlations have been converging in the modern era.
3. Canadian and US companies already offer a

global footprint in their businesses.

We have already discussed the first point in the previous section on US Stocks, but the other two points require a bit of explanation. There is some recent academic and mathematical evidence that states global stock markets are moving more in tandem with each other. We saw this in the 2008 crash, where stocks fell worldwide. With our interconnected world, a financial crisis will affect everyone at once. Having stocks in Australia did not save the North American investor in 2008. Rather, having bonds with a negative correlation would have provided greater safety to the overall portfolio – when one goes down, the other goes up.

The third point is that the kinds of companies you are getting by buying an American index are already global in their nature. The largest stocks on the list – Apple, Microsoft, Amazon, etc. are not solely American, but international companies themselves. Even members of the 6-Pack Portfolio, like Scotiabank have a large presence in Latin America. Often these companies will be better equipped to take advantage of regional growth than the domestic companies in emerging markets – who have a higher likelihood of corruption and inefficient management. If we look to the developed world, most of the stocks are in Europe and Japan, which both suffer from low economic growth.

All told, I believe International and Emerging Market stocks are more trouble than they are worth for the Canadian investor. But if you insist on hedging your bets, it could offer some extra diversification as a small allocation in your overall portfolio. The ways to invest would be the aforementioned VEA (developed) and VWO (emerging) ETFs on the NYSE. Alternatively, you could buy VXC on the TSX in Canadian dollars, which holds every stock market in the world except Canada, meaning that you could complement it with the 6-Pack Portfolio.

Bottom Line

- International and Emerging Market stocks make up the rest of the world market outside Canada and the USA. Although not a barometer of future returns, they have performed very poorly in recent times.
- Investors may choose to avoid these stocks for many reasons, including global stock market convergence and the international nature of many North American companies.
- If wanting to get access to these markets via ETF, VEA offers exposure to International Stocks, while VWO holds Emerging Markets.

Precious Metals

Gold, silver, platinum, and palladium are precious metals and considered their own investment class. For enthusiasts and experts, it would be worth following the markets for all of these metals. But the average investor can get away with only one: gold.

For thousands of years, gold has been king when it comes to being a store of value and recognized form of wealth. It is not currency in a sense anymore, but can easily be exchanged for currency at a predictable exchange rate. More than stocks, bonds, and especially cash it stands the test of time – for instance, an ounce of gold can buy you a nice designer suit whether it is the year 1818 or 2018. If there was a chest of items buried in a vault since the 17th Century: a bar of gold, a stock certificate, and paper dollars – likely only the gold would hold its value, as the paper dollars become worthless due to inflation, and stock in a company would almost certainly have long since been made obsolete by a merger, bankruptcy, or fundamental shift in the market.

Aside from its store of value, gold is also a solid additional to a portfolio based on its low or negative correlation with the stock market. The same cannot necessarily be said of silver, platinum, and palladium, which as industrial metals have some correlation to how the economy is doing. Gold is often seen as a flight to safety; when faith in the economy or the government is eroding, the price of gold tends to rise or at least stay steady.

Having the yellow metal in your asset mix will level out volatility, and be a welcome relief for your portfolio during stock market turbulence as it was during 2008. Gold is also a great place to be during inflationary or deflationary periods: in the inflation-heavy 1970s gold was the best performing asset class, and during deflation in the 1930s its purchasing power rose while the prices of most other goods fell.

One aspect of gold that can be both a positive and a negative is that it is not affected by the performance of any one company or manager. Gold is just gold – atomic number 79 on the periodic table of elements, and that is all it will ever be. As such, it can be a bit more predictable in its pricing behaviour than a specific stock would be. Although it is not normally recommended to time the market, with precious metals you can apply some logic and make some short-term allocation decisions or trades if you so desire. I will show an example of what I am talking about in the following chart:

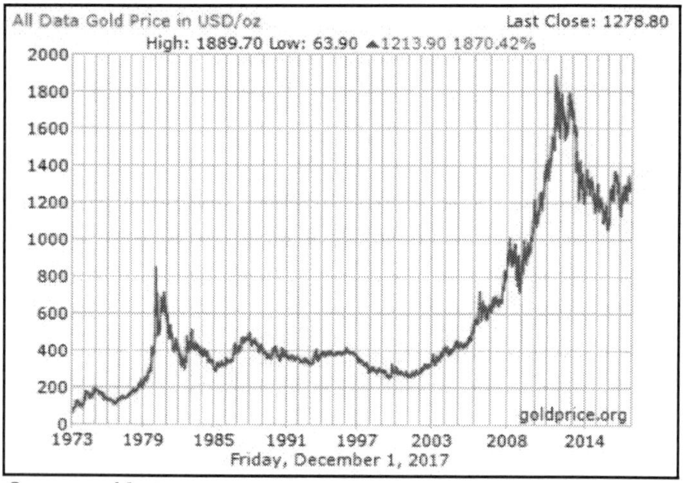

Source: goldprice.org

The chart shows the price of gold roughly since President Nixon removed the US gold standard in 1971 during the "Nixon Shock". What we can infer from the past is that there was a big run-up in gold during the late 1970s that culminated in a peak price of $850 USD per ounce in 1980. The subsequent crash and bear market consolidation period lasted for 20 years, coinciding with a bull market in stocks. Then, in recent history when gold had a decade-long bull market and reached a peak price of over $1,900 an ounce in 2011, it also crashed and has been languishing around $1,200 to $1,300 per ounce since then.

I'm sure you can see where we are going with this line of thinking – if history repeats itself, then gold may not enter another bull market until around 2030. This sort of analysis isn't just assuming the future will be the same as the past, it also coincides with the cyclical nature of markets. I believe it will take a while for gold to build up a head of steam again, it needs time to consolidate for another bull run. That's why there's not necessarily a hurry to get into gold if you do not own some already – but one can slowly start to add it to your portfolio in preparation for the next bull run and for diversification purposes.

It is difficult to say when the start of a bull market in precious metals will be, but the end is easy to spot. Once the average person starts talking about and asking you about gold, and the price hits the news headlines daily, that's when it's time to lighten your exposure in preparation for another crash. Once the average person has bought, there is no one left to buy and that leaves the price nowhere to go but down.

So, how do you invest in gold? To get its full benefit, which includes protection from disaster or a general failing of the system as we know it, the best way is to own physical gold. 1oz Canadian Maple

Leaf coins are .9999 pure gold, and are attractive to look at too. These can be purchased from a bank (Scotiabank is the most gold-friendly) or a reputable coin dealer.

If you are uneasy about owning physical gold and storing it safely, it can be purchased via an ETF that tracks the price of gold, at a small annual cost. There are some products on the TSX that you can look into if you wish – such as CEF.A which also has a silver component. But I would recommend GLD on the American market as it is the oldest and most liquid ETF for gold investment. To easily get US Dollars at a small or non-existent exchange rate, read the next chapter in this book!

Alternatively, you can purchase companies that mine gold and other precious metals. The Canadian market has the largest selection of gold miners in the world, with big names including Goldcorp (G), Barrick Gold (ABX), and Agnico Eagle Mines (AEM). The best performing name has been Franco-Nevada (FNV), which has a royalty and streaming model rather than outright mining.

I would argue against owning miners, especially large ones, for reasons already stated in this book. They deplete their source of revenue, and it gets harder to find every year. Better to own the resource itself, which lasts forever. They also perform terribly in normal market conditions, and have been a large reason why the TSX has been easy to beat for the 6-Pack Portfolio in the last seven years. However, if you're interested in trading it may be worth looking into holding a few smaller miners during a gold bull-run.

Silver is also an interesting trade during a precious metals bull-run as it tends to rise faster than gold. The counterpoint is that it crashes faster and harder when the run is over. Its volatility and its more positive correlation with stocks is why I wouldn't recommend it as a major asset in your allocation. If you get the physical version, there are also storage concerns because you need so much of it to have significant value. Most investors can safely stick with gold.

Bottom Line

- Gold fits strongly into a portfolio as a store of value, a hedge against instability and inflation, and for its low correlation to stocks.
- As a commodity, gold is driven by cyclical bull and bear markets and may not enter another bull market for a decade or so.
- Buy 1oz Canadian Maple Leafs for access to physical gold, or GLD on the NYSE for virtual storage. Avoid gold miners in a long-term portfolio.

Bonds & Cash

Bonds and cash are in a pretty bad place right now. With the 10-year benchmark Government of Canada bond yielding ~2%, fixed income represents a very poor return on investment. Even with the magic of compound interest, holding a 2% interest 10-year bond to full term would only net you $2,190 on an investment of $10,000. And if it is outside of a registered investment account, you would even be subject to taxes on that measly profit. Assuming you bought the bond inside a TFSA or RRSP and interest rates stay the same, it would still take you a full 35 years to double your money. Nobody has time in their short life for that kind of investment. So, with interest rates so low now, are bonds and cash really worth your time?

It really depends on your specific situation. If you are young with stable employment, it doesn't make much sense to put a lot of money in fixed income. If you are already retired or nearing retirement though, the extra safety for your overall portfolio may be necessary. As is the case with gold, bonds benefit from a negative correlation with the stock market.[3] Unlike cash or GICs which merely hold their value, the price of bonds rise during poor economic times or when interest rates fall. In 2008, they performed even better than gold and saved many portfolios from gut-wrenching volatility.

[3] Note that sometimes this negative correlation turns positive, in cases where the bond and stock market fall together. In this event, cash is king.

But this safety comes at a cost, because when interest rates rise or when the economy is doing well, the price of bonds tend to fall and they will be an overall drag on your portfolio. In the long-run, the price action isn't as important, and you can expect to earn whatever the yield to maturity (YTM) is on the bond or bond fund.

In the current interest rate climate, I combine bonds and cash into their own asset allocation. Bonds now represent what I would call a medium risk and low reward investment. If interest rates rise faster than expected, their prices will suffer. Therefore, it's worth thinking about moving a lot of that would-be bond money into cash, which is no risk and low reward. As I mentioned previously with gold, it could be beneficial to slowly add more weight to bonds as interest rates rise and the economic cycle turns in their favour. They have had their bull run since the 1980s, there isn't much room to run any further.

So, where to put your allocated bond and cash money? Cash can be a regular high interest savings account at your bank, or an investment savings account with your brokerage. I like to add all dividends received into the RBF2010 Investment Savings Account with RBC Direct Investing to squeeze every last cent out of my accounts. At higher interest rates, Guaranteed Investment Certificates (GICs) can be an attractive option if you don't mind locking in your money. For bonds, I would recommend buying an ETF for diversity and simplicity sake. VAB or XBB represent options on the TSX, holding a mix of mostly government bonds at a variety of maturity dates. VLB or XLB represent longer maturities that align with the Permanent Portfolio philosophy outlined in the next section.

Bond funds can also perform a bit better than their yield to maturities would suggest, as they benefit from what's called "riding the yield curve" – basically selling bonds before they approach maturity and purchasing longer term bonds at a higher yield. There is all sorts of math and research that goes into the bond market, and globally it is even larger than the stock market. But personally, I am holding my excitement until interest rates reach at least 4%.

Bottom Line

- Bonds benefit from a low or negative correlation with the stock market, and can help your portfolio ride out market volatility.
- At current interest rates, Bonds & Cash should be kept liquid and not be a major portion of your portfolio unless your age or financial situation calls for it.
- Investment Savings Accounts or general savings accounts are a good place to keep cash. VAB/XBB are good general bond ETFs, with VLB and XLB as long bond options.

Sample Asset Allocations

Having gone over the different asset classes, we can now look at some sample allocations to consider when constructing your own investment portfolio. Basically, we'll be putting all the pieces together like a jigsaw puzzle.

In this section I will be using a handy backtesting tool for Canadian investors on the Stingy Investor website, located at http://www.ndir.com/cgi-bin/downside_adv.cgi. Note that past performance does not translate into the same thing happening in the future; especially the bull market in bonds since the 1980s would be near impossible to replicate. But it does give you an idea of how the asset mix you have chosen will behave throughout the economic cycle. We will start our look at different portfolio options with one of the best.

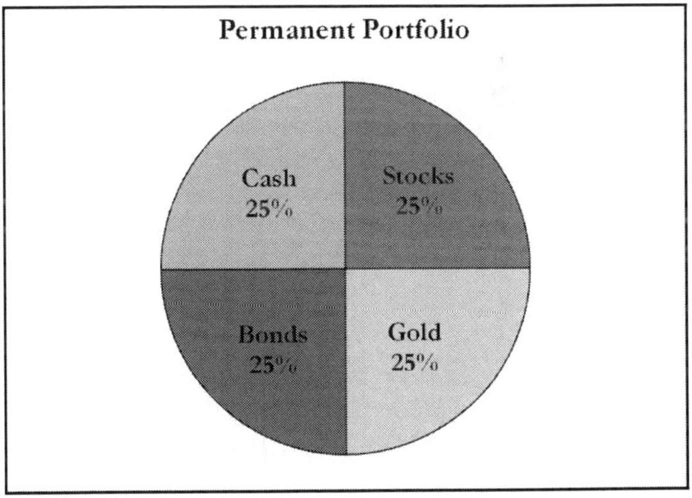

My first exposure to investment philosophy was with Harry Browne's Permanent Portfolio. His idea was to split your assets into four equal portions: Stocks, Bonds, Gold, and Cash. The concept is to have an asset that benefits during all possible economic scenarios, whether it is Prosperity (Stocks), Recession (Cash), Inflation (Gold), or Deflation (Bonds).

As we know, this mix of assets is good for diversity sake due to the low correlation among its components. He recommends long bonds for that portion due to their even lower correlation and higher interest rates. Conventional investment academia says that everything about this portfolio is wrong: the high weight in gold, the high weight in cash, and the exposure to long bonds rather than medium term. The reality is that this portfolio has very low volatility, and its long-term performance holds up.

In my backtesting of the Permanent Portfolio, I have assumed 3-month Canadian T-bills for the Cash portion, Canadian Long Bonds for the Bonds portion, and a 50/50 split of the TSX Composite and S&P 500 for the Stocks portion. The results are astonishing. Since 1970, there has only been 2 down years for the Permanent Portfolio. In 1981, the portfolio lost 5.95%, while in 2013 it lost an insignificant 0.06% – essentially even. The average gain over that time has been a respectable 9.432%, meaning that a $10,000 investment in the Permanent Portfolio in 1970 would be worth $691,565 today.

Perhaps the biggest benefit of the Permanent

Portfolio is protection of capital. For peace of mind, this asset mix is a great choice. In 2008 when the sky was falling for a lot of investors, the Permanent Portfolio actually had a small gain of 1.48%. If this doesn't end up being your own allocation, it can at least give you an idea of how different asset classes can work together over time. The wisdom of Harry Browne lives on.

Although the Permanent Portfolio has shown great protection and growth of capital since 1970, there are some concerns with that allocation when looking to the future. Given that current interest rates dictate that any Cash allocation can expect to earn about 1%, and any Bond allocation can expect to earn about 2% in the near future, the Stock and Gold allocations would have to earn a phenomenal annual return to get anywhere close to an aggregate 9.43% portfolio return as in the past. And even if that happened, you would be wishing that you had taken more risk in your asset allocation.

Another problem: this book is meant to get you excited about the 6-Pack Portfolio, and under the Permanent Portfolio structure those stocks would only make up a mere 12.5% of your total holdings if you split your Stocks allocation between Canada and the US. Hardly enough to make a meaningful impact. Therefore, I propose an alternative asset allocation for you to consider:

Advanced Asset Allocation (AAA)

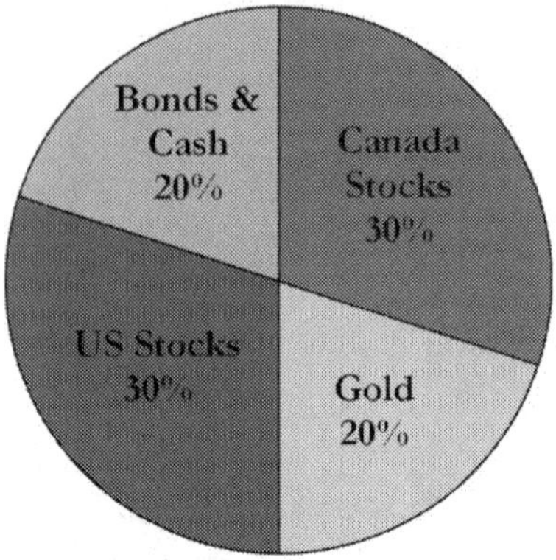

The Advanced Asset Allocation (AAA) is my preferred asset allocation for Canadians throughout most stages of their investment lifetime. It is an allocation that I have personally created and tested. It takes the best aspects of the Permanent Portfolio and adjusts it for the modern age, with some logical synergy between the four components. Basically, you could say that the asset mix has a 60% risk component from the Canada and US Stocks, with a 40% safety component from Bonds, Cash, & Gold.

But there is more to it than that. We have already seen how the 6-Pack Portfolio is complemented well by a US Stock index in terms of sectors, so the risk components are nicely diversified. Gold has some correlation with the Canadian market because we live in an economy that depends on exporting its commodities. But the Bonds & Cash component can safely balance the risk from the 6-Pack, while the Gold component is a nice offset to US Stocks due to their low or negative correlation with each other.

Furthermore, your Canadian Stocks, and Bonds & Cash will be priced in CAD, while the US Stocks and Gold will be likely be priced in USD. So, you can easily have half of your total portfolio in Canadian Dollars, and half of it in American Dollars for simplicity sake. I will show you in the next chapter how to get USD cheaply, so do not worry about that.

The Advanced Asset Allocation is designed with a look to the future, as investors have to cope with lower interest rates. But it has also performed well in backtesting. This asset mix has more risk than the Permanent Portfolio, but also more reward. There were six down years between 1970 and 2016, with the worst decline of 10.49% coming in 2008. But the average gain was a healthy 10.22%, meaning that the same $10,000 investment in 1970 would have grown to $968,735. This is noticeably higher than the $691,565 earned through the Permanent Portfolio, despite 10.22% not seeming to be much higher than 9.432% annual return. The compounding effect really makes the extra return show over long periods of time.

We can compare the Advanced Asset Allocation with a portfolio that an average US investor may consider with similar 60/40 risk and safety components. 40% US Bonds, 40% S&P 500, and 20% International Stocks (as represented by the MSCI Europe Asia and Far East Index) is a conventional asset mix. This specific portfolio had a lower return than our AAA equivalent, 10.011%

annually since 1970 for a final value of $886,021.

But the volatility and risk of that conventional portfolio were also much higher. There were seven total down years, with the largest drop of 19.91% occurring in 1971. Although that is only one more down year than the Advanced Asset Allocation, many of these drops took a long time before getting back to even. The portfolio lost money in 2002 which took 4 years to recover from, while another loss in 2007 took another 5 years to recover from! After a brutal period like that, many people would have sworn off investing forever.

By comparison, only one of the money-losing years from the Advanced Asset Allocation took longer than one year to recover from – the two-year period of 2001 and 2002 where the portfolio lost around 7% and 4%. Protecting from downside and recovering from drops quickly is a surefire way to keep yourself invested and protect your financial psychology. With this overall allocation as your investment strategy, you could say that you have AAA-rated protection!

If you find yourself not resonating with my preferred asset allocation, that is okay as well. You can customize your own allocation as you see fit. This can include removing Gold if you do not believe in precious metals, adjusting your Fixed Income allocation and adding International Stocks for example. But whatever you do, make sure you believe in your plan and are able to stick to it through all kinds of market conditions.

Bottom Line

- The Permanent Portfolio's mix of Stocks, Bonds, Gold, and Cash helps protect your capital by having a mix of assets that can perform throughout the economic cycle.
- The Advanced Asset Allocation (AAA) has 30% Canadian Stocks, 30% US Stocks, 20% Gold, and 20% Bonds & Cash. It works well with the 6-Pack Portfolio as the Canadian component. It also takes on more risk than the Permanent Portfolio, with the potential for more reward.
- All logical asset allocations and portfolio designs should be made to reduce your risk and increase your reward. One key consideration is recovery after a loss – how many years does your portfolio take to get back to even?

CHAPTER 5
IMPLEMENTATION

At this point, you have been introduced to a method that has beat the performance of the Canadian stock market, and also presented with some asset allocation ideas for investing your overall portfolio. The next logical question that you may have is how do you actually put these ideas into place? A great plan isn't worth much if you cannot execute it.

This chapter will focus on the logistics of setting up your investment portfolio – everything from TFSA's, RRSP's, and online brokerages, to actually buying the shares. Some of this may be review or redundant for those who already have self-directed investments. But I have also included some valuable rules of thumb for how to get the most out of your portfolio that may not be common knowledge, and some useful tips including how to get American dollars at a low cost. First, we will look at the two main investment accounts in Canada: the TFSA and RRSP.

Tax-Free Savings Account (TFSA)

The simplest investment vehicle with tax benefits available to Canadians, the Tax-Free Savings Account (TFSA) began in 2009 as a means to incentivize saving in Canada. As the name implies, most capital gains, dividends, and interest earned within this account are tax-free. But despite the "Savings" moniker, the TFSA is best used to hold investments.

Residents of Canada who are 18 years or older build up annual contribution room. The starting amount in 2009 was $5,000 and has been indexed to inflation in $500 increments since then, excepting one year in 2015 when the Conservative government set the amount to $10,000. This information is probably easiest to digest in table form:

Year	TFSA Annual Limit	Cumulative Limit
2009-2012	$5,000	$20,000
2013-2014	$5,500	$31,000
2015	$10,000	$41,000
2016-2018	$5,500	$57,500

Source: Canada Revenue Agency

This means that if you were born in 1991 or earlier and have lived in Canada at least since you turned 18, then you have access to the full $57,500 in contribution room available on January 1, 2018. If you became a resident of Canada or turned 18 in 2017 on the other hand, then you would have $11,000 in contribution room. And so on. Note that there are penalties for overcontribution, and although the CRA has records of your contributions and withdrawals it is best to keep track of them yourself.

Think of the TFSA like a hotel. You can check-in money anytime up until your total contribution limit, and check-out money anytime as well which gives you that contribution room back. But if you are at the total contribution limit, then you cannot re-check that money in until January of the next calendar year. If this information is not sinking in yet, that's normal. All the rules and explanations are readily available online, so what we'll focus on ahead is strategies on how to get the best out of the account.

When deciding what to do with your TFSA contribution room, inevitably you will compare its structure to your other investment vehicle options – often the RRSP. The RRSP provides the investor with tax-savings upfront in the form of a rebate by lowering your income, and then your later withdrawals will be taxed at your marginal rate. On the other hand, your TFSA contributions will be after-tax dollars, so you get no rebate upfront, but you also pay no tax on your withdrawals. Therefore, it would be best to put your highest growing assets in the TFSA – that way, there is no painful taxation when you want to withdraw large amounts later in your lifetime.

When thinking about your different assets, high

growth generally means stocks. The TFSA's best use is as a harbour for your Canadian Stocks – namely, the 6-Pack Portfolio. The growth and dividends that you receive for these holdings can grow tax-free within the account, and you don't have to worry about them at all when filing your taxes. This is beneficial when you consider some potential holdings in your portfolio like the REITs pay 'return of capital' in their distributions, meaning that if held outside a tax shelter they can be paperwork burden come tax-time, especially if you sell your shares many years later.

So, the TFSA is great for Canadian Stocks, but what about equities based in other countries? Unfortunately, the US government does not consider the TFSA a retirement account in the same way it does an RRSP, so US Stocks and holdings in a TFSA will have their dividends affected by an annoying withholding tax. Furthermore, if you are a US resident or dual-citizen who files a tax-return with the IRS, the TFSA is subject to all sorts of scrutiny and taxation that defeats the purpose of the account as a tax shelter.

We've established that the TFSA is best used as a holding for Canadian Stocks. So, let's look at a concrete example. Take a person with $100,000 to invest who was born in Canada in 1991 or before, and has never contributed to their TFSA. Using the Advanced Asset Allocation (AAA) as a guide, they would want to allocate 30% of their holdings to the 6-Pack Portfolio. That means $5,000 apiece for a stock in each of the six sectors and a total of $30,000. The rest of their contribution room could be used for Bonds, but gradually shifted to Canadian Stocks as the overall portfolio size gets bigger. Gradually meaning the investor is not making trades so often that the trade commissions start to add up.

If and when your portfolio gets much larger, you may have the problem of not having enough room in your TFSA to house your 6-Pack Portfolio. In this case you could move some of your holdings into your RRSP if you have a lot of room there, or into a non-registered account. Make sure if you have stocks in an unregistered account that they pay wholly eligible Canadian dividends or have no distribution at all, which is most stocks other than REITs.

My own personal strategy for my TFSA is to build it up to a million dollars over time, and hold solely the 6-Pack Portfolio stocks within it. Given that the 6-Pack has a goal of 4% dividend yield, the TFSA would then provide me with $40,000 of income tax-free every year!

As a final note on the TFSA, I want to emphasize just how powerful tax-free growth can be. After reading this you will want to get the best out of your registered accounts right away. Consider the example of someone contributing $10,000 to their investment account every year for 30 years. Assume their money grows at an annual rate of 7%, and that their marginal tax rate is 30%. The difference between investing this money within registered accounts (RRSP/TFSA) and non-registered accounts is staggering.

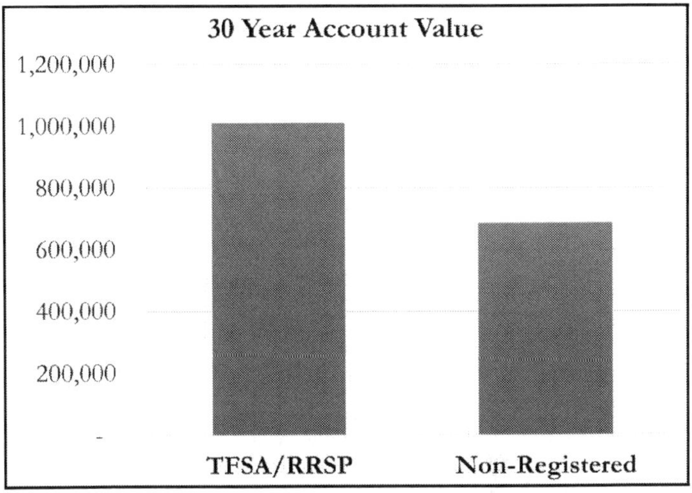

Despite investing in the exact same securities, the tax-sheltered accounts beat non-registered handily. After 30 years, the registered investments grew to $1,010,730, while the non-registered account grew to $685,093. If having an extra ~$325,000 sounds appealing to you, I don't blame you. Take advantage of tax-free investments as soon as you can!

Bottom Line

- Pros: The TFSA is a great vehicle to grow your investments free from taxation, with simple and flexible deposit/withdrawal rules. Great for younger Canadians who have time to build up a lot of contribution room.
- Cons: The TFSA is not well suited to holding US stocks, and is not recommended for US citizens and those who file taxes with the IRS.
- Recommendation: Use your TFSA to house

Canadian assets with steady growth and income like the 6-Pack Portfolio. Bonds can be placed here as well if you do not have RRSP room or do not need to open one yet.

Registered Retirement Savings Plan (RRSP)

More well known to Canadians in the pre-Millennial generations, the Registered Retirement Savings Plan began in 1957 to promote saving for retirement in Canada. For those who grew up with the simpler and more flexible TFSA option to save and invest, the RRSP can be a bit harder to understand.

Instead of every Canadian earning a set contribution room annually, i.e. $5,000, your RRSP gains contribution room based on your reported income to the CRA. 18% of your income is added to your cumulative contribution room; for instance, if you earn $100,000 in a year, then $18,000 will be available in the RRSP. There are annual contribution limits, but these only come in to play if you make over $140,000 per year. The easiest way to check the room available to you is at the bottom of your latest tax return, or through the CRA online system.

Unlike the TFSA which is almost a no-brainer to use and invest within, the RRSP requires a bit more planning. While contributing to and withdrawing from a TFSA is almost a non-event, with the RRSP contributing and withdrawing both have special rules. Contributions reduce your taxable income, so if you make $60,000 annually and contribute $5,000 to the RRSP, your taxable income will go down to $55,000. Your next tax return will be adjusted accordingly so that you get a rebate for taxes paid on that $5,000 you earned.

Furthermore, when you withdraw from your RRSP, the amount you take out will be treated as income and taxed at your marginal rate. You may also get additional fees depending on the institution your RRSP is held with. It is for these reasons that money within this account should be considered locked away until you retire.[4] Once you turn 71, the RRSP can no longer be contributed to. Your account can then be converted into a Registered Retirement Income Fund (RRIF) to still receive tax sheltering for your investments, but you will be forced to withdraw from it annually.

As a general rule, to maximize the value of your RRSP, you should be contributing to it when your personal income is high, and withdrawing from it when your personal income is low – like during most people's retirement. Contributions can be strategized based on tax brackets. For instance, if you make over $91,831 in 2017 those extra dollars will be taxed at 26% rather than the 20.5% of the previous federal tax bracket. If you make $100,000, it may be worth contributing ~$9,000 to your RRSP in order to

[4] One exception is for the first time Home Buyers' Plan, which you can read about here: https://www.canada.ca/en/revenue-agency/services/tax/individuals/topics/rrsps-related-plans/what-home-buyers-plan.html

reduce your income and be rebated for the higher taxes you paid. There are also different provincial tax rates on your income based on where you live within Canada to consider.

A big negative of the RRSP in my eyes is that it is so tied to your reported income. Take time off to go to school, get money from family or inheritance, or make your living through other means like by way of a corporation – and you do not earn contribution room. Furthermore, there are many variables, including your future income and future tax rates that are essentially unknown. But, as a registered account, you can count on one main advantage that the RRSP offers – years of tax-free growth on the investments within it.

Now, let's discuss what investments make the best sense within the RRSP. As mentioned previously, American securities are not subject to withholding taxes on income earned within an RRSP, as the US Government considers it a retirement account with special privileges. For that reason, it makes sense to hold your US Stocks here – if you go with my recommendation, either SPY or VTI to cover the whole market. One fund for all of your US holdings, easy. There are also some Canadian stocks that pay dividends in USD, like Algonquin Power & Utilities (AQN). It would make sense to keep any stocks like these in your RRSP, and include their dividends in your future purchases of US index funds.

The RRSP is also particularly well-suited to holding Bonds. You do not want to hold fixed income in an unregistered account, as the interest is fully taxed at your marginal rate. Bonds also do not offer spectacular growth, with no long-term capital gains and small interest nowadays. So, it will not hurt as much when you withdraw from your RRSP in retirement. An example: invest in Bonds within your RRSP to reduce your taxes, then use the tax rebate to invest in Canadian Stocks within your TFSA. That's definitely making the most out of your accounts.

Bottom Line

- Pros: The RRSP is a great way to shelter investments from taxation until retirement, and as a means of reducing taxation for high-income Canadians. It also holds status as a retirement account in the eyes of the US Government, avoiding withholding taxes.
- Cons: The RRSP is not very flexible when it comes to depositing and withdrawing, so money put in should be considered locked away. Money is taxed when it comes out, so it is not as good as the TFSA when it comes to higher growth investments.
- Recommendation: Use your RRSP to house US Stocks and Bonds. You can hold VTI from the NYSE and VAB from the TSX. You could also hold GLD here if you are investing in gold and keeping most of your US Dollars in your RRSP. Two or three holdings in your entire RRSP. Easy.

Non-Registered Account

A non-registered account is an investment account you can open which is not protected from taxation. If you buy and sell securities in this account, you will be subject to capital gains and losses, and any passive income earned, i.e. dividends and interest, will have to be accounted for on your tax return. If you keep all of your investments non-registered, after a while it may start to become a nightmare to keep track of at tax time. So, why bother with one of these accounts?

There are a few reasons to consider opening a non-registered account. For one, if you are a fortunate Canadian who has managed to maximize the contribution room in both your RRSP and TFSA, you may not have another choice for a place to house your liquid assets. In that case a non-registered account is just fine, but it is important to place the right investments in it.

A non-registered account is the best place to hold speculative investments. Your losses can be offset by future or past capital gains. This means that if you lose $2,000 in one trade and make $2,000 in another trade, you are even and pay no taxes. But if you lose $2,000 in a trade and do not gain in any other trade, then you can carry forward that loss to subsequent years, where hopefully you will have some gains to apply that $2,000 loss towards.

Therefore, it makes sense to hold speculative securities in a non-registered account, whereby you are just as likely to lose big as win big. An example may be a small mining company, technology or health care company, or options contracts. Notice that I do not recommend these sorts of buys in my example asset allocations, but I know that many people tend to deviate from their plans occasionally for some speculation. That's fine, as long as it isn't a major part of your portfolio.

If you have a large portfolio and have maxed all of your registered accounts, a non-registered account may also be the right place for some of your 6-Pack Portfolio stocks. These stocks pay eligible Canadian dividends, meaning they have preferential tax treatment. If eligible Canadian dividends are your only source of income, for example in retirement, then you can earn a certain amount – close to $50,000, before they are taxed at all. The specifics I cannot comment on because I am not a tax expert and they are liable to change every year. Remember though, to keep stocks like REITs and others that distribute return of capital within registered accounts, so you do not have to keep track of the extra accounting.

Bottom Line

- Place speculative investments within non-registered accounts.
- If you have maxed your TFSA and RRSP, consider placing some 6-Pack Portfolio stocks in non-registered accounts, i.e. Banks, Railroads, Telecoms.
- Do not place Bonds and other fixed income in

non-registered accounts as they are taxed as full income.

Registered Education Savings Plan (RESP)

If you have children, or are planning to do so in the future, the Registered Education Savings Plan is a great way to save for their education. There is no annual contribution limit, but there is a lifetime maximum of $50,000. There are two major benefits of the RESP: tax-free growth within the account, and the Canada Education Savings Grant (CESG).

The CESG grant is basically 'free money', whereby the federal government will supplement your investment into your child's RESP by 20%. For example, if you invest $1,000 into the RESP, the government will grant you an additional $200. There is an annual limit of $500 for this grant (this can be higher if you have low income), and a lifetime limit of $7,200. Therefore, to get the most out of the CESG, annual contributions of $2,500 and lifetime contributions of $36,000 would earn the maximum government grants. If you invested $2,500 every year until your child turns 15, that would do the trick.

When it comes time to withdraw the RESP funds for your child's education, the tax considerations are fairly straightforward. Everything that you have contributed is withdrawn tax-free, while the CESG grants and investment gains are taxed. Consider the case that you contributed $36,000 over the years, had CESG grants of $7,200 and investment returns of

$10,000. The $36,000 would be withdrawn tax-free, while the $7,200 and $10,000 would be taxed. Remember that the latter money was also subject to many years of tax-free growth, which is very beneficial.

The investments placed inside an RESP would likely look much different than your personal investment account. I would advise on going much more conservative with your asset allocations. In fact, I don't think there is much reason to take much risk at all. The investment time horizon is much shorter with the RESP, especially if you do not start contributing to it when your child is a baby. Although it's best to invest early, you may only start thinking about an RESP when your child goes to school at around 5 years old. By then, there's only about 12 or 13 years left until they are university age. Any turbulence in the stock market would be hard to come back from.

Some RESP investment advice states that you should start with a large portion of the portfolio in equities, then gradually decrease the risky assets until you are 100% Fixed Income when your child is 18. This could work fine. But I would personally be quite conservative from the start and include a substantial Fixed Income portion. This is what I plan to do with *my own newborn daughter's account.*

Given that the government is adding in a guaranteed 20% bonus on my investment contributions, low interest rates don't bother me so much. I have been negative on Bonds & Fixed

Income in previous chapters, but they really work better here. As is, a conservative portfolio will already be low-risk and relatively high-reward. No sense in messing with that, and I can sleep easy at night.[5]

So, what securities should you invest in within the RESP? For the Fixed Income portion, you can go with bond funds until they are a teenager, and then laddered GICs after that. If you're adding a little bit at a time, like $50 per paycheque, then it would make sense to go with a low-cost mutual fund. A well-known example are the TD e-Series funds, which have lower expenses than traditional mutual funds (0.50% MER for the Canadian Bond Index). If you plan to add lump sums annually to the RESP, then a Bond ETF like Vanguard's VAB (0.13% MER) would make sense.

You may also decide to invest in an equity component within your RESP portfolio. The additions to the account will likely be too small and frequent to replicate the 6-Pack Portfolio here. The TD e-Series funds also offer Canadian, US, and International equities, which can be paired with the bond fund in desired percentages. An example allocation could be 50% Bonds, 25% Canadian, and 25% US Stocks. You know I am not a fan of the TSX index, but for passive investment options of this

[5] Note that the 20% added return is on the contributions, not the total account value. So the effect of the government grant on the total account return will be smaller over time percentage-wise.

account size you don't have much of a choice. As an overall allocation, the Permanent Portfolio would also work well here as it preserves your capital.

We haven't discussed Guaranteed Investment Certificates (GICs) much yet in this book, mostly because they are not an exciting investment for a normal portfolio at current interest rates. But when your children or grandchildren start to approach university age, they make sense. A GIC locks your money with a bank or other institution at a set interest rate for a certain length of time. Generally, the longer the timeframe the higher the interest rate. The principal is guaranteed so you cannot lose money like you could in a bond fund.

If your child is 13, then setting up a 5-year GIC ladder within their RESP would have their cash ready for university. The 5-year ladder works like this: split the investment into five equal parts, and invest those amounts in GICs maturing in 5, 4, 3, 2, and 1 years. When the 1-year GIC expires, invest that in a 4-year GIC, and so on. Eventually all of the money will mature at the same time, and you may have benefitted from rising interest rates. You could also ladder the GICs so that they mature each year at the time when tuition is due. If you don't grasp this concept right away that's fine, as your bank will be happy to sell you on it. Alternatively, you could just purchase one GIC maturing when your child graduates high school, but this limits flexibility and increases interest rate risk.

We have talked about the RESP, and some potential investment strategies that you can employ within it. But as an aside, it is worth discussing the value of an expensive education in today's world. Paying top dollar for an education, and then expecting to land a dream job in 4 years time is a very 20th Century concept. In a globalized world moving towards automation every day, the job market for young people is tough despite their education levels. There are social and networking benefits to going to university, but nowadays in the YouTube era, so much can be learned online for free just by searching for it. It is still worth investing in the RESP, but keep an open mind as to how the world will look in the future.

<u>Bottom Line</u>

- The RESP is great for saving for a child's education, with a lifetime limit of $50,000 in contribution room and a maximum of $7,200 available in government grants.
- With a limited time horizon and guaranteed government grants of 20%, it makes sense to invest in a lot of Fixed Income within the RESP, giving your portfolio low-risk and high-reward.
- In a child's early years, invest in bond funds such as TD's e-Series option for regular contributions, or ETFs such as VAB for lump sum contributions. When they are a teenager, you can invest in a GIC ladder.

Online Brokerages

In previous chapters and sections, we have outlined specific investments, investment strategies and philosophies, and what type of investment accounts to open. But in order to hold investments, you will need a brokerage to act as your foothold in the market. For simplicity sake you could go with the brokerage that your personal bank offers, or you could look into some other options available.

There are a couple of resources online that provide detailed comparisons and rankings of the online brokerages in Canada. Rob Carrick from the Globe and Mail has an annual ranking, as does the Money Sense website. I will not give links because by the time you read this there may be a more current version, but both are easily accessed on Google. Luckily for us, most of the brokerages offer fairly cheap trading nowadays – the standard is about $10 per trade.

One brokerage that I do recommend for investors just starting would be Questrade. They have cheaper commissions than the big banks – usually $5 per trade. But the great thing is that they offer free purchases on any ETFs. That means you could add to the holdings of your US Stock, Bond, or Gold ETF anytime for free, and not have to worry about commissions eating up a portion of your trade. You will have to pay a commission to sell, but if you are a long-term buy and hold investor, that should not matter so much. Later on in your investment career when the difference between a $5 or $10 commission doesn't matter, you may want to switch to your personal bank brokerage for convenience.

Once you have a brokerage account with money inside it, the next step is to buy shares. It is a simple concept. If you have $5,000 set aside to buy CN Rail stock, and the stock is trading at $100 per share, then you will want to buy 50 shares of CNR on the TSX. The numbers aren't usually that even, so make sure to leave a buffer for commissions and price fluctuations. You can usually buy any number of shares you want if it is a well-known and liquid security, but if it is more thinly traded you may want to purchase the shares in multiples of 100 (lots) to ensure fulfillment.

Make sure to set your buys as 'limit orders', as the 'market orders' could be risky for more thinly traded stocks. Setting a limit order means the highest price you are willing to buy. Standard practice is setting the limit buy below the 'bid/ask', i.e. if the bid for the stock is $55.50, you could set your limit buy at $55.48. A lot of times I don't personally have patience for that, as I'll be watching the price move around and might not get filled for a while, or at all. So, I'll set my limit buy to something like $55.55 instead to ensure a trade (the broker will still fill at the best price available). That way, you still have the protection of the limit, but don't have to mess around with your bids. Unless you're dealing with vast sums of money, a few cents won't make a difference anyway.

Bottom Line

- Research online for the brokerage that's right for you. The Globe and Mail and MoneySense have annual rankings and comparisons.
- Choose Questrade if you are a new investor and dealing with smaller amounts (under $50,000).
- Make sure to use limit orders when buying and selling securities.

Exchanging US Dollars for (Almost) Free

We have talked about how sample asset allocations require you to hold US Dollars in order to purchase specific funds – namely VTI for US Stocks, and GLD for tracking gold. You can create a diversified portfolio with only Canadian dollars though. For instance, VUN on the TSX gives you exposure to the US market priced in Canadian dollars, while VXC gives you exposure to the rest of the world outside Canada, including the USA. I do personally prefer the products listed on the NYSE though. The big reasoning is the extremely high liquidity, coupled with assurance that the broker won't short-change the investor on currency exchange for dividends.

That brings us to our next point, why do we want to find a way to exchange US dollars that's different from the default one our bank gives us? Because the banks take a percentage of your conversion as fee for the exchange. Typically, this is about 1.5% of the exchanged amount. That means, for a conversion of $10,000 CAD to USD, you would immediately lose

$150 to hidden fees in the exchange. And if you wanted to convert that money back to CAD, you would lose another $150.

This extortionist and hidden practice by brokers can be combatted by the technique known as Norbert's Gambit – named for Norbert Schlenker of Libra Investment Management who popularized the method. The gambit takes advantage of arbitrage and is basically this – to get US Dollars, you buy an interlisted stock on the TSX and instantly sell that same stock on the NYSE. Interlisted stocks are those that appear on both the Canadian and American markets; the best examples are the big banks, i.e. TD and RY. If you wanted to convert USD back to CAD, just buy the American version of the stock and sell the Canadian version. You can trust the market to price these stocks on the TSX and NYSE at exactly the given rate of exchange between the CAD and USD.

In any case, when you do Norbert's Gambit, the only cost of the trade is the commission plus or minus any minor movements in the market as you are completing the maneuver. So, for an average brokerage it would be $10 to buy the interlisted stock, and $10 to sell it. That $20 cost is much less than the $150 you would normally pay your broker.

If you are uncomfortable with trading the interlisted stocks, there is an even easier way to do it: with DLR and DLR.U. These are simple ETF products from Horizons that track the price of the US Dollar, with DLR in Canadian Dollars and

DLR.U in US Dollars (the latter should always stay around the same price). To convert CAD to USD, buy DLR and sell DLR.U, and vice versa. Although you are more protected against market movements with this method, you will have to pay a bit of a bid/ask spread cost to Horizons along with your commission.

Gambitting is easier to do at some brokerages than it is to do at others. Google Norbert's Gambit for specific instructions at your brokerage. Some brokerages require you to journal the interlisted shares from the Canadian to the US side of your account and vice versa. If you do not have a brokerage yet, consider choosing one where this method is easier to do at. It helps if your account allows you to hold US Dollars directly. RBC Direct Investing has very easy gambitting, for example.

Bottom Line

- Brokers charge a hidden fee, on average about 1.5%, for converting CAD to USD.
- Use Norbert's Gambit to get USD for the cost of two trading commissions. The easiest way is to buy DLR and sell DLR.U.
- Check online if there are any quirks with your specific brokerage and account type for executing the gambit.

CHAPTER 6
SUMMARY

We have reached the sixth and final chapter, an appropriate number considering the title of this book! In this section, I'll try to put everything together as a summary of what has been outlined so far, and as a template for actionable investing. If you're convinced about the logic within these pages and want to start putting money to work, there's no better time to start than now. To illustrate the process, I'll use the example of an investor with $100,000 to invest.

Step 1: Determine an Asset Allocation

Our investor is a 30 year old Canadian with no children, so they still have a long way to go until retirement. That means they can take some investment risk with their asset allocation. But there is no need to take unnecessary risk, and that is why a strong portfolio with assets that have negative or low correlation is so powerful. Diversification is a free lunch, so you may as well eat it up. Different assets within the portfolio will balance each other out, and prepare the investor for all types of economic situations: prosperity, recession, inflation, and deflation. For our asset allocation, we will go with the Advanced Asset Allocation:

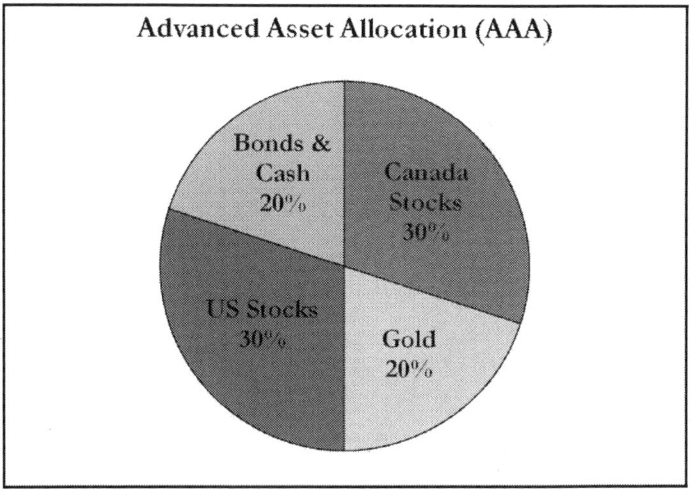

After doing some simple math, our investor would buy $30,000 in Canadian Stocks, $30,000 in US Stocks, $20,000 in Gold, and $20,000 in Bonds & Cash. This allocation can be maintained through new purchases, and rebalanced annually if necessary.

Step 2: Setup Investment Accounts

The second step for our investor is to open the appropriate investment accounts to hold the chosen assets. Given that in this example, the investor is 30 years old in 2018, then they are eligible for the full $57,500 in TFSA room. For simplicity, let's say that they have also earned $57,500 in RRSP room through their income over the years. At this point, the investor can utilize both of their registered investment accounts without going over the limits.

Our investor decides to open their registered accounts with RBC Direct Investing because that is where they do the majority of their banking. Now, they must decide what assets go in which account. As explained in the asset allocation chapter, Canadian Stocks, as represented by the 6-Pack Portfolio, are a great fit for the TFSA, while US Stocks are best in an RRSP – $30,000 in each.

So, the only question is where to put the $20,000 in Gold and $20,000 in Bonds & Cash. Contribution room dictates that one will have to go in the TFSA and the other in the RRSP. You could make arguments for putting either one in either account. Although Bonds are perhaps best placed in an RRSP long-term, the investor may opt to place them in the TFSA for now, with the Gold in the RRSP. The main reasoning is that the TFSA can house Canadian Dollar items, with the RRSP holding US Dollar items.

So, we have our plan: $50,000 in the TFSA to be split between Canadian Stocks, Bonds & Cash, and

$50,000 in the RRSP split between US Stocks and Gold. The latter $50,000 can be converted to US Dollars within the RRSP using Norbert's Gambit. See the last chapter on how to do this maneuver.

Step 3: Purchase Securities

The next step is the most fun, purchasing the stocks and ETFs that will make up your portfolio. For our theoretical investor with $100,000, it might look something like this:

Location	Stock/ETF	Symbol	Amount
TFSA	TD Bank	TD	$5,000
TFSA	CN Rail	CNR	$5,000
TFSA	Telus	T	$5,000
TFSA	Fortis	FTS	$5,000
TFSA	Enbridge	ENB	$5,000
TFSA	CAP REIT	CAR.UN	$5,000
TFSA	Cdn. Bond Index	VAB	$20,000
RRSP	Total Stock Market	VTI*	$30,000*
RRSP	SPDR Gold Trust	GLD*	$20,000*

**Note: NYSE purchases will be in USD equivalent, i.e. if CAD is at 0.80 USD, then these amounts will be $24,000 for VTI and $16,000 for GLD in USD.*

I believe the above portfolio provides a great blueprint for the average investor in Canada. It has the strength of the 6-Pack Portfolio, and the risk reduction of asset diversification. No one stock makes up more than 5% of the overall portfolio, reducing specific company risk. At the same time, there are only nine holdings in total, easier to manage than a lot of the smorgasbord-style portfolios that some individual investors end up with.

Step 4: Maintain and Rebalance

Once you have your portfolio set up, prudent investors will keep an eye on it to make sure it is still aligned with their asset allocations and goals. Our 30 year old investor is in their prime earning years, so new income will be coming in every year if all goes well. One can use this new income to top-up the underperforming categories of their portfolio, forcing a buy-low investment strategy.

However, be careful not to make purchases too often, as that can be inefficient in terms of trading commissions. Once a year purchases are likely often enough for the 6-Pack Portfolio, perhaps aligned with new TFSA contribution room in January. So long as your percentages are reasonably close to your planned asset allocation, there is no cause for alarm.

Closing Notes

The above steps give a condensed version of the investment process, and how the plans laid out in this book can fit into it. If this specific example does not align with your situation or goals, it can be customized accordingly. Remember that this is not solicited investment advice, and I gain nothing from you buying these specific stocks. I am just a regular retail investor who has found success in the market through building logical portfolios, and want to share that knowledge with you.

I hope you have found this book useful, and have learned more about the Canadian stock market and investing in general. When you think of the best method to beat the TSX, think of the 6-Pack Portfolio. It's okay to make money! I wish you good luck and good fortune in your investments.

All the best,

Jason Fremlin

ABOUT THE AUTHOR

Jason Fremlin's passion is turning money into more money. He has been investing in the stock market since 2010, beating the TSX index return every year. His goal is to pass that knowledge onto Canadians, and help them reach their long-term financial aspirations.

Jason has an MBA degree from the University of Victoria. He lives in British Columbia with his wife Veronika and daughter Grace. Reach out to him directly at jason@bluefoot.ca.

48478831R00061

Made in the USA
Lexington, KY
16 August 2019